TYNE
AND
WEIRD
II

First published 2022

The History Press
97 St George's Place, Cheltenham,
Gloucestershire, GL50 3QB
www.thehistorypress.co.uk

British Library Cataloguing in Publication Data.
A catalogue record for this book is available from the British Library.

ISBN 978 1 8039 9096 5

Typesetting and origination by The History Press
Printed in Great Britain by TJ Books Limited, Padstow, Cornwall.

MIX
Paper from
responsible sources
FSC
www.fsc.org   FSC® C013056

TYNE AND WEIRD II

ROB KILBURN

ILLUSTRATED BY DAN UNDERWOOD

The History Press

This book is dedicated to my son, Oliver Andrew Kilburn.

I dedicate this book to you knowing that though you entered this world at a strange time, you inherited the strength of your mother, Sarah, the creativity of your father and the combined love of us both.

I hope in the years to come you reflect on this strange tome and inherit the curiosity and caution with which it was written.

I also dedicate this book to my little brother, James Kilburn. Not so little anymore but still looking out for his family and brother. I cherish your support and the strength you have given to me and our family.

CONTENTS

FOREWORD

Greetings travellers!

Welcome once again to the paper embrace of the collection of eclectic tales that is *Tyne and Weird*.

Going back to my youth, I remember being thirsty for tales tall and small, in particular ones involving the paranormal or themes on the fringe. From urban legends of the customer who finds a fried rat in her fast food, to the friend of a friend who has returned from travelling abroad with strange spots on her lips – only for it to be later revealed that those particular spots can only be acquired from kissing someone who has been in physical contact with dead bodies.

One particular tale I remember hearing that related to the North East was that of a taxi driver who, returning from a fare late one night on a country road, passes a woman looking disheveled and distressed. He pulls over and offers to drive her to safety, though he cannot get much sense from her. During the journey he looks back in the rear-view mirror expecting to see the sobbing woman, only to discover his taxi is empty with no trace of that passenger ever having been there.

Stories like this tend to have a life of their own, being adapted from one person to another having happened to their relative or a friend, and eventually the origin disappears like a mumbled word in a game of Chinese whispers.

The stories included in this book are the very same and will hopefully take on a life of their own upon entering your head.

Whether you are telling a friend in the pub or cracking on with a relative at Christmas over dinner, embrace these tales and fulfil their purpose by spreading the word.

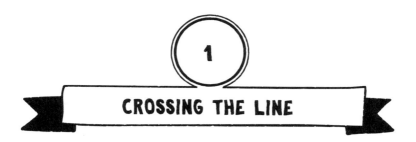

CROSSING THE LINE

If we could all run around doing whatever we wanted, I dread to think of the consequences and the kind of world we would live in. That privilege is reserved for the rich, but the people in these tales, like you and I, cannot live without consequence.

The stories you'll read in this chapter detail what happens when you cross that legal line, whether right or wrong by modern standards. I ask you, the reader, to put yourself in the shoes of the desperate men and women that committed these crimes.

GRAVE ROBBING AT CHRISTMAS

On Christmas Eve 1823, not everyone was in good spirits. Captain Hedley of Sunderland had a sad task to undertake: the burial of his 10-year-old daughter, Elizabeth.

It was a cold winter and the icy weather in Sunderland parish graveyard had frozen the earth, so much so that the ground could not be properly dug. Unable to penetrate to the usual depth, a shallow grave would have to suffice.

Four sad days passed and the captain wanted to move his daughter's body to a better part of the graveyard. No doubt this would have been the only thing on his mind for the four days over Christmas, sullying what is the happiest time of the year for most. Determined, he returned to the graveyard only to find that the child's coffin was bare.

The authorities were alerted immediately and upon investigation they reached the conclusion that the body of his 2-year-old daughter had also been stolen from its tiny coffin.

GRAVE ROBBING AT CHRISTMAS

The authorities were not without suspects, though, and they turned their focus to two strangers who had been seen lurking around the cemetery, particularly at times when funerals were taking place. The police acted quickly and one of the men was apprehended that afternoon.

Word had got out of the foul deed committed by the two strangers and an angry mob soon formed. While being transported to the police courtroom, the baying crowd threatened to stone the man to death. Terrified by the idea that the police may hand him over, he began confessing to the crime.

Constables were sent immediately to the lodgings of the man and it was there they found the criminal's fellow grave robber, who was in possession of the body of Captain Hedley's daughter. Packaged in straw, the body was ready for delivery to an address in Edinburgh.

Upon further investigation, the police found human teeth and various documents linking the two men with the removal of six bodies.

It became clear that the fiends had been robbing graves throughout the whole county. The men had been sending the bodies further north by horse and cart to Scottish surgeons. The two criminals would be identified as Thomas Thomson of Dundee and John Weatherley of Renfrew.

The next month, January 1824, the two Scotsmen took the stand at the Durham Sessions, pleading guilty to the offence of grave robbing.

While you might expect such a despicable crime to carry a heavy sentence, the two men received very lenient sentences. For their crimes they received just three months' imprisonment, together with a fine of sixpence.

HUNG, DRAWN AND QUARTERED

In January 1593, Newcastle would be home to the grizzly execution of a Roman Catholic priest. Until the start of the 1530s, English Christianity had been under the supreme authority of the Pope. King Henry VIII, after having his annulment to Catherine of Aragon denied by the Pope, declared himself Supreme Head of the Church of England and began having the monasteries closed down. Shortly after, Catholicism would become illegal in England for a period of over 200 years. This is when our story takes place …

Edward Waterson was born in London and raised in the Church of England. His adventurous spirit would see him cross the waters and travel through Europe to Turkey with some English merchants, where he no doubt would have been exposed to a wide variety of cultures and customs. Upon his return to England, Edward stopped in Rome, where his faith would turn to the Catholic Church and he would be ordained as a priest in 1592.

Deciding to return to England would not have been a frivolous decision because of the danger to his life for just being a Catholic priest, but it is one he decided to pursue regardless. Upon arriving in his home country another Catholic priest aboard the same ship, Joseph Lambton, was arrested but Edward had a very lucky escape.

His fortune soon turned, however, as he would be captured less than a year later in midsummer 1593. Joseph, the fellow priest aboard his ship coming to the country, had been executed in 1592 and the sheriff is said to have shown Edward the quartered remains in an effort to frighten him. Regarding these as holy relics, Edward showed no fear and would languish in jail until after Christmas, when he would be executed as a traitor.

He was brought to Newcastle to be executed, but things would not go according to plan. When he was being brought to his place of execution, the horses carrying him refused to move, forcing him to be brought on foot. This unfortunately did not save him and he would undergo the horrific process of being hung, drawn and quartered.

For those of you who may have forgotten what you were taught at school in relation to this particular method of execution, let me remind you. Reserved for the most serious of crimes, the process would begin with the convicted person being brought to a wooden panel by horse, where they would be hanged until almost dead. Just as relief of the noose no longer being around their neck would set in, they were emasculated, disemboweled, beheaded and then chopped into quarters. The remains were often placed aloft in areas where the public could easily see them so as to be a constant reminder of what happens to those who committed such serious offences.

Father Edward Waterson, being recognised as a martyr, was beatified by Pope Pius XI in 1929.

THE ART HEIST

A retired bus driver from Newcastle, who at the time was also a disabled pensioner, I might add, is not the kind of person you might think would be likely to be responsible for one of the most notorious art thefts in Great Britain ... but then again you may not have heard the name Kempton Bunton.

Born at the turn of the century in 1900, it would be many years before his name would surface in the media alongside the word *thief*. Having retired from his job, Kempton was living on £8, which left little funds for himself to use at his discretion. In the 1960s a painting by the renowned Spanish artist Francisco Goya of the Duke of Wellington was to be sold to a rich American art collector, and to be taken to his home back in the United States.

It was at this point that the British Government intervened to keep the painting on British soil, paying the same amount offered by the buyer of £140,000 (the equivalent of over £3 million in today's money). Kempton was said to be enraged at this, living on the little money he had and still having to pay for a TV licence.

Kempton has said that through simply talking to the guards at the National Gallery he learned a lot about their complex security system, which involved infrared sensors, alarms and a number of other electronic security protocols designed to keep some of the country's most treasured works of art safe. This would be enough to deter anyone thinking of pilfering the art ... that is, of course, if the systems were active and not actually switched off in the morning for the cleaners ... which they were.

On 21 August 1961, Kempton had allegedly wedged a bathroom window open and slipped in, leaving with the prized painting in hand via the same window. The police assumed that an experienced art thief had performed the daring criminal act but a letter was then sent to Reuters news agency with a demand that £140,000 be given to a charity that would pay for TV licences for poorer people alongside amnesty for the theft, a demand that was not met.

Four years would pass until 1965 when Bunton contacted a newspaper and, just like in a spy movie, the painting was returned via a lost luggage office in Birmingham. Bunton then turned himself in to the police, admitting theft. During the trial he was only charged with the theft of the frame in which the painting was held, as he returned the painting itself and never intended to keep it.

While he received three months in prison, it was later revealed that it may well have been his sons that were involved in the initial theft and then passed the painting to their father. Bunton, the bus driver from Benwell turned art thief, died in 1976, leaving behind the question of who really took that painting from the National Gallery.

THE HIGHWAYMAN

Gateshead Fell in the eighteenth century was an area with a reputation for being a danger to those unaccustomed to it, and one such local character named Robert Hazlett no doubt took his share of the blame for this reputation. Hazlett was a highwayman who would chance upon coaches passing by and rob them at gunpoint.

This unfortunate career choice would be the end of him when he perhaps got a little greedy and attempted to rob two people in one night on the vast marshland of Gateshead Fell in 1770. His greed saw him rob a woman named Ms Benson, whom it is said reported the highwayman to a mail carrier making his way down the road following her escape from the scene. The mail man did not listen and crossed paths with Hazlett who, much to his later regret, also robbed him, committing a crime now punishable under the Murder Act of 1752, which permitted gibbetting for those caught.

Hazlett was destined to face the law and was eventually caught and taken to court. In an astounding turn of events, it seems that Hazlett had even robbed the judge who was to give him his sentence at some point, giving him little chance of any mercy. He was hanged and his body gibbetted by

THE HIGHWAYMAN

a local pond as a deterrent for all those who might be tempted to pursue the same career. John Sykes touches on this in his book of local records:

> Hazlett's gibber, or stob, as it was called, remained here many years after the body had disappeared. On the in closure of the Fell, Hazlett's pond (which was the name it retained from the circumstance of the gibbet), becoming the property of Michael Hall, Esq., that gentleman caused the pond to be drained and cultivated.

FURIOUS RIDING

In our long recorded history, we have criminalised and legalised many a strange thing. What is legal today might be illegal tomorrow and vice versa.

Reported in the *Sunderland Echo* in 1935 is a case where a group of men received a fine for a bicycle-related crime. Below is the report:

> Fines of 10s each were imposed at Sunderland County Petty Sessions to-day on John Bramley (20), Outram Street, Sunderland; Enoch W. Smith (22) of Mailings Rigg, Sunderland; Joseph Sanders (20) of Henry Street, Hendon; and James Miller (32) of Trewhitt's Buildings, Sunderland; for riding furiously.

How does one ride furiously exactly? Were they going too fast? Being reckless? Or did their face bear an angry expression? I am afraid I cannot answer that question for you. While it is still illegal today to ride your bicycle under the influence of alcohol and other substances, I can't see anyone being charged with riding furiously anytime soon.

HIGH TREASON

Nicholas Emil Herman Adolphus Ahlers was living in Roker, Sunderland, when the First World War broke out. He was most likely a well-recognised and respected man, having worked at the German Consulate in Sunderland. In 1914, on orders from his home country, he was tasked with recruiting German men that were of fighting age to return overseas.

Ahlers was arrested and his office was searched, revealing a number of documents that linked him to the departure of local Germans. When he was brought to trial, a number of his countrymen testified against him, including Otto William Martin, of Tunstall Road, who described being approached on a tramcar in Roker and being advised to return home or face consequences. Ahlers's defence argued that he was unaware of the announcement of the outbreak of war between the two countries and had only been soliciting people for a few hours following this. Soon after this he was found guilty of high treason in Durham and sentenced to death.

One particular quote from Ahlers at his trial that newspapers repeatedly shared was this: 'Although naturalized, I am German at heart.' His verdict was appealed successfully as anti-German prejudice was found to have occurred during the trial. Shortly after being released, he moved down south and began going by the name Anderson while under watch from the Government. Both Ahlers and his wife were eventually interned and were kept separate from each other.

While detained in Holloway Prison in 1917, Emma Ahlers, Nicholas's wife, committed suicide. She had been struggling to cope with the separation that her family now faced and was also unable to sleep. In a letter left under her pillow she asked for forgiveness from Nicholas and detailed her belief that their children would look after each other. Nicholas Ahlers was eventually deported back to Germany in 1919.

THE FATAL TRAIN ROBBERY

On 18 March 1910 two men boarded a train at Newcastle at the start of a journey that was destined to change both their lives. John Innes Nisbit boarded the 10.27 service from Central Station bound for Stobswood Colliery in Northumberland to deliver £370 in wages. When the train reached the end of the line, Alnmouth Station, his body was found

THE FATAL TRAIN ROBBERY

under the seat, having been shot in the head five times, with the bag of money missing.

Witnesses' testimony pointed to a man named John Alexander Dickman, a local bookmaker, who had also been on the train. Dickman never denied being on the train and he explained that having become distracted reading his newspaper he had missed his stop, for which he paid the excess fare. Described by some as a professional gambler, it is believed he had recently encountered money problems, giving some cause to believe he had motive for the robbery and killing. He was soon arrested and evidence against him began to mount up as more witnesses tied him to the scene. After missing his stop, he got off and attempted to walk to the station but reportedly said he became tired part of the way and returned to the station he departed at.

It was revealed that two different cartridges from different guns were found on or near the body of John Nisbit, suggesting to some that there may have been two killers. Dickman's home was searched and neither the guns nor money was found, although the money bag was later located down a mine shaft near Morpeth. Dickman's suits were clean, but a stain was found on his raincoat that remained unidentifiable. Contradictory evidence as to Dickman's guilt made the result of the trial even more shocking when the verdict came back that he was to be sentenced to death.

In this story I have only touched on some of the evidence that made this case one that history has remembered. It has been retold on Orson Welles's *The Black Museum* as well as numerous times on the BBC, in recent years in the programme *Murder, Mystery and My Family*.

Despite a public appeal, John Alexander Dickman was sentenced to death and was one of the last men to be hanged at Newcastle Gaol on 10 August 1910.

BIZARRE BODY PARTS

At the beginning of 2021, Northumbria Police received an alarming call that a dog walker had uncovered human remains in a muddy field at

Winlaton, Gateshead. The startled member of the public had seen what they believed to be a human toe poking out from the ground and had alerted the authorities.

This triggered a large-scale response in search of the body with numerous police units and dogs attending the scene. Upon finding what was believed to be a human toe, police unearthed it further and realised that it was actually a very unfortunate looking potato, or a potatoe if you will, much to the relief of everyone.

Another similar tale from 1884 tells how a human leg had washed up on Tynemouth beach, causing great alarm. Speculation arose, with some saying the leg belonged to a man and others saying a woman, but all had agreed it was a horrid murder and that a body had been dismembered for quick disposal. The explanation it seemed was even stranger because it turned out that a local gentleman had a bear presented to him, which was slaughtered and cooked to eat. A leg was given to the head of the family as a luxury but, not satisfied with the bear flesh as a meal, it was wrapped in cloth and thrown over the cliffs, only for it to wash up and have the appearance of a human limb.

PRIVATEERING OFF SHIELDS

Privateers were a force used by many countries in the 1700s and 1800s to undertake guerrilla warfare tactics at sea. Merchant ships were authorised to conduct raids on the ships of a country with which their government was at war. One such example of this was the French privateers, who were called Corsairs, and at the time of this story in May 1779 they were permitted to carry out pirate-like activity off the coast of the North East due to our poor relationship with France at this time.

Early one Sunday morning a number of ships sailed from Shields and had not got very far out to sea when they encountered one such small fleet. Numerous ships were taken hostage and offered back to England for ransom, with onlookers standing on the coast actually being able to watch in shock as this happened. Armed ships at the harbour did set out in pursuit of the offenders, with some being peppered with ammunition from the privateers. The thieves of the sea escaped with a hull full of cargo on this occasion, leaving a community rattled by the prospect of setting sail.

CRIME AND PUNISHMENT

Justice is something that can mean different things to different people. While some crimes considered serious many years ago are now something you might get a slap on the wrist for, back then the consequences would be dire. Digging through old records can uncover some fairly tragic tales, like that of John Scott, who in 1802 was hanged in Morpeth for the crime of sheep stealing, or William Alexander, who in 1783 was hanged on Newcastle Town Moor for committing forgery.

Over the years our idea of punishment has also changed. Take, for example, the drunkard's cloak, sometimes referred to as the Newcastle Cloak. With drunkenness becoming a crime in 1500s, this strange punishment was a barrel from which a hole in the top was carved, thus allowing a person's head to fit through while the barrel remained covering their body.

One early description of the drunkard's cloak being used here in the North East appears in Ralph Gardiner's *England's Grievance Discovered*, which was first published in 1655. A gentleman, John Willis, claimed to have travelled to Newcastle and seen the following:

> Men drove up and down the streets, with a great tub, or barrel, opened in the sides, with a hole in one end, to put through their heads, and to cover their shoulders and bodies, down to the small of their legs, and then close the same, called the new fashioned cloak, and so make them march to the view of all beholders; and this is their punishment for drunkards, or the like.

I think many of us in the North East are partial to a good drink every now and then but I dread to imagine how many barrels we would see rolling around should this punishment still be in effect.

Another long-gone punishment is to be pilloried and thrown at the mercy of the public. This usually involved a wooden framework where the person's head and arms would be put through and they then became imprisoned and suffered the wrath of public abuse. Cases of this in the North East have been recorded for crimes such as perjury, such as in 1758 when Susannah Flemming was pilloried for fortune telling, or again in 1791 when a woman was pilloried for perjury in Sandhill, Newcastle.

This may seem like an archaic method of punishment and perhaps something better suited to the Middle Ages but it wasn't all that long ago that this was used, with the last recorded case in Sunderland in 1811. It would not be until 1837 that the pillory was completely abolished as a punishment, fewer than 200 years ago.

PRESSING MATTERS

While for many years hanging was the capital punishment for those deemed Britain's worst offenders, there have been many other methods that have been used. One such is to be pressed to death, which is simply another term for being crushed. The guilty party would be spread out, often with separate ropes tied to their hands and feet, and a big sheet of metal or wood placed over them. From here the agonising process of slowly increasing the weight on top of the surface would begin with rocks being loaded up, putting immense pressure on the subject. Death would not be immediate and this process could sometimes last days while the unfortunate person's bones were slowly crushed along with their organs until the body could not take any more.

One case of this happening in the North East occurred in Durham in 1578. The punishment was often reserved for those who would not plead innocent or guilty, making them uncooperative to the crown. Thomas Green was one such case and he was pressed to death on Palace Green in August 1578 as a recalcitrant witness, enduring an agonising death.

FORCED LABOUR

In Houghton-le-Spring lies the small village of Fencehouses, which has an interesting rumour regarding its name. During the Napoleonic Wars it is said French prisoners of war were held here and it was originally named Frenchhouses, which later became Fencehouses.

While this is very much up for debate, what is reputedly known is that French prisoners from the Napoleonic Wars were used as labour to dig out the Houghton Cut, which now has a road running through it that leads to the A1.

MISSING PERSONS CASE

Miss Mamie Stuart was a young Sunderland lass who had dreams of becoming a stage dancer. In 1918 it looked like she was headed for domestic bliss and married a marine engineer named George Shotton, who whisked her away to live in Wales. It would not be long, though, until she would seemingly disappear from the face of the earth.

The last contact she would have with her family was Christmas 1919, when she was 26. Soon after they would report her missing. Her husband was immediately suspected and during the course of their investigation it would emerge that George had married Mamie bigamously, for which he would serve a prison sentence.

The trail went cold, but sightings of Mamie would surface now and then, sometimes even in different parts of the world, although she was never located. In 1961 a set of bones and some jewellery were uncovered in an abandoned mineshaft on the Gower peninsula in Wales and these were later identified as belonging to her.

George Shotton had since died and his involvement could not be proven. Mamie's remains were stored in a laboratory until a Mrs Oldnall, whose grandmother was Mamie's sister, was approached by American television channel CBS Reality to appear in a programme based on the story. During this Mrs Oldnall, with the help of forensic pathologist Dr Stephen Leadbeatter, recovered the remains and had them returned to Sunderland.

Mamie's body was returned to her family after going missing 100 years ago and is now buried in Bishopwearmouth Cemetery alongside her father and mother.

ONE-ARMED BANDIT MURDER

This notorious murder of Angus Sibbet took place on 4 January 1967. Michael Luvaglio and Dennis Stafford met Sibbet at the Birdcage club in Newcastle at 12.30 a.m., 16 miles away from the eventual scene of discovery of Sibbet's body. Sibbet was discovered in his Jaguar on 5 January, having been shot three times.

The case was one of the most notorious gangland killings in the North East and sparked fears that organised crime was taking a foothold. The following trial resulted in life sentences for Stafford and Luvaglio.

Both men had protested their innocence, with Luvaglio alleging it was part of a failed attempt by the Krays to enter the Newcastle club scene. Both men were released on licence twelve years later.

The film *Get Carter* starring Michael Caine and set in Newcastle took inspiration from these real-life events.

Did you know that the infamous British gangsters the Kray twins paid a visit to Newcastle? There is even photographic evidence of the two brothers sat at a table at the La Dolce Vita nightclub in Newcastle in the 1960s along with heavyweight boxing champion Joe Louis.

A ROOFTOP CHASE

Robert William Hall was a small-time crook who was deported from America for violent crimes. Hall served a fourteen-year prison sentence in Sing Sing Prison in New York for a shooting in Chicago and for threatening police with a razor during a break-in at a hotel.

Hall, who also went by the aliases Robert Dodds and William Jones, was a street musician who played his violin in Newcastle. In the early hours of 29 August 1932 police were alerted to a burglary at the Benwell Hotel. Hall and an accomplice had tried to break in via the glass roof of a toilet, only to be pursued across the rooftops.

Hall desperately attempted to shake the police by knocking over a chimney pot, going so far as to throw slates at the police and the gathering crowd of spectators below. At one point he lost his footing and fell from the roof, fracturing his skull. He was taken to Newcastle's Royal Victoria Hospital, where he was pronounced dead.

A TALE OF BIGAMY

Robert Taylor was a young man who on 29 June 1840 was tried for bigamy in Durham. Taylor, who also called himself Lord Kennedy, was found to have had at least six wives of which the police were aware. It is believed he was aged between 19 and 21 and had wives all over the country. During the trial, family members provided testimony to knowing the man and being present at the weddings.

Two years after his trial in Durham he was caught again after marrying a woman named Foster, and was sentenced to fourteen years' imprisonment.

Did you know there was once a tax in England called the Window Tax, which was first imposed in 1696? Houses were taxed on the number of windows they had, much to the frustration of the urban working class. As a result, many people bricked up their windows to avoid paying the strange tax. The Window Tax was abolished in 1851 but next time you are walking around the city centre and see a bricked-up window, this tax may well have been the reason why.

GRAVE ROBBING IN THE 1980S

It was a dark night at the start of the winter of 1984 when the soil was being disturbed at Westgate Hill Cemetery in Newcastle. A group of young men calling themselves The Gentlemen of the Club had entered the graveyard under the cover of darkness with one motive … to dig up graves.

The unusual event resulted in five young men taking six bones and nine skulls back to their home, where the story gets even stranger. The gang had an interest in experimental music and the remains of the long deceased were destined to become musical instruments. Thigh bones had holes drilled into them to create Tibetan thigh trumpets, which they believed that when blown into released the souls of the dead, while other bones would be used for drums. Although the men denied being involved in occult practices when they were arrested, in one of their homes skulls on an altar, books on magic and a stuffed seagull were found.

The group of five men, who had released some music online under the name Metgumbnerbone, admitted removing bones from three graves and desecrating the remains of ten people, which included the bodies of men, women and children. A manuscript was kept detailing their dark deeds, which described how at midnight the group went to the graveyard with shovels and flashlights. The following is an excerpt from the document:

> It was not a long walk to our goal. And once there we speculated as to where at first we should strike.
>
> On what piece of ground should we first lift the spade to the earth. Name, sir, which grave that man has made to incarcerate.
>
> Christian, in undisturbed rest, sent in tomb to lie in peace, inviolate, shall we in turn violate?
>
> Our destination, which you will perceive, was to the cemetery given into the parish of Elswick.
>
> Here we did find our first objective. A crypt belonging to a family.
>
> It had been much labour to shift the uppermost piece of brickwork upon which the grave slab rested.
>
> They had lain unmolested for 130 years …

Dark stuff indeed but the men did pay the price for their actions, with some of the gang serving time in jail for their strange crimes. I think it is important to remember, however, that during the 1980s we were going through a big cultural shift, with the likes of the Temple of Psychic Youth gaining momentum. Religious and spiritual beliefs were changing in society and perhaps these young men had imaginations too big for their own good.

EDICT OF EXPULSION

Now here is a bit of English history I imagine is unfamiliar to many of us, although perhaps it should be better known.

In 1209 the Edict of Expulsion was issued by King James I of England that expelled all Jews from the Kingdom of England. Although Jews were likely to have resided in England as far back as the Roman occupation, they were now ordered nationwide to leave the country under an increasing atmosphere of anti-Semitism.

With tragic massacres occurring in places like York in 1190, where 150 Jews were massacred during anti-Semitic riots, growing hostile conditions faced the community and led to an exodus for many years. This led to very few Jews remaining in England through the entire Middle Ages, with the decree itself only being overturned more than 350 years later by Oliver Cromwell. Hence Jews were only allowed to return and settle in England in 1657. Even with the decree overturned, it would be another 100 years before the first Jewish congregation would be formed in Sunderland, and possibly the North East, in 1768.

THE CHOPPING BLOCK

Sir John Fenwick, 3rd Baronet, was born in 1645, the eldest son of Sir William Fenwick, patriarch of a prominent Northumberland family. Starting his career in the army, he quickly rose to the rank of major general and would come to be a strong supporter of King James II. By the time William III had control of the throne after the revolution of 1688, Sir John had run into money problems and had gone as far as selling off part of his inherited estate.

Believing James to be the rightful King of England, Sir John began to plot to overthrow the new King William, even being jailed for a short period of time. Upon his release, he renewed his efforts and schemed to assassinate the royal.

When his fellow conspirators were captured, however, Sir John lived on the run for a period of time before ultimately being arrested under charges of treason.

While in the King's custody, he feebly attempted to save himself and began telling all he knew of the Jacobite plots and fellow conspirators, although these would ultimately prove inconclusive. While in jail his friends had managed to remove some of the witnesses in his case in an almost Mafioso-type fashion, giving him hope that the charge of treason would be dropped due to a lack of evidence.

This was not to be the case, however, and Sir John would be the last man to be executed under the Act of Attainder, ironically an Act that he had initially supported.

He was to be beheaded and was brought from prison to a scaffold at Tower Hill, London, his head forced down upon a block and the executioner, given the signal, separated his neck from his head in one foul swoop of his axe. Due to his aristocratic heritage, his execution was well documented with a great crowd said to have attended. Having handed over a paper containing some detailed information and his last thoughts, he forgave the executioner who was soon to end his life, and is reported to have met his end without any notable last words spoken.

His severed head and body were then taken to St Martin-in-the-Fields during the night, where he was finally laid to rest. The below is an excerpt of a letter he requested to be delivered to King William once his sentence had been carried out:

> If there be any Persons whom I have Injured in Word or Deed, I heartily pray their Pardon, and beg of GOD to Pardon those who have injured me; particularly, those who with great Zeal hath

sought my Life, and brought the guilt of my Innocent Blood upon this Nation, no Treason being proved upon me.

I return my most hearty Thanks to those Noble and worthy Persons who gave their Assistance, by opposing this Bill of Attainder; without which, it had been Impossible I could have fallen under the Sentence of Death. God bless them and their Posterity; tho', I am fully satisfied, they pleaded their own Cause while they defended mine.

A FRAUDULENT MEDIUM – NEWCASTLE, 1905

Christopher Chambers was a touring medium in the North East of England who claimed the ability to make spirits materialise. One particular performance in Newcastle cast major doubts on his abilities and led to his reputation being destroyed.

A local man by the name of Mr Neale was not convinced of Chambers's claim to possess supernatural powers. During the performance the medium climbed inside a cabinet while the lights were dimmed and a pale spirit rose up into the air. Neale had been prepared for this moment and turned on two electric lamps, which revealed the medium shrouded in a sheet and wearing a paper turban. The audience's fury at the illusion led to everyone's money being refunded and subsequent reports in the papers did much damage to his reputation.

A photograph with Christopher and a spirit also circulated around that time but proved to be fake when Newcastle photographer James Wallace sent a letter to the *Newcastle Daily Chronicle* admitting the forgery. The Newcastle Society for Investigation of Spiritualism, formed in 1872, also investigated his powers only to conclude him a fraud. Christopher then travelled down to London to be tested by the Society for Psychical Research and prove his abilities. These tests also went terribly for Christopher as he was observed moving objects himself and at one point wearing a fake moustache.

When the SPR released their findings, Chambers denied all counts of fraud but agreed to never work as a medium again. It is believed, however, that upon his return to the North he continued his practice.

BURNT AT THE STAKE

Nicholas Ridley was born in 1500 into a prominent family in Tynedale, Northumberland. During his youth he was educated at the Royal Grammar School in Newcastle, before furthering his education at Pembroke College in Cambridge. Following this he became a priest in the 1520s and travelled to Paris to continue learning before returning in 1529.

Through his education, Ridley was considered well versed in Biblical hermeneutics, the study of the principles of interpretation concerning the books of the Bible, and he joined the debate on the supremacy of the Pope as church leader in England. Ridley had become Proctor of the University of Cambridge in 1534 and under his influence the university argued 'That the Bishop of Rome had no more authority and jurisdiction derived to him from God, in this kingdom of England, than any other foreign bishop.'

Ridley continued to further his career, obtaining notable positions and furthering his education, even beating a charge of heresy in 1543. During the reign of Edward VI he was appointed Bishop of Rochester and then Bishop of London. However, when the young King became seriously ill in 1553, Ridley's controversial thinking would prove his downfall. His support for Lady Jane Grey as the next succeeding monarch over Edward's Catholic pro-Pope sister Mary, something supported by the King, would prove fatal. Ridley issued a proclamation that Mary and her sister Elizabeth were illegitimate; however, when Edward died in 1553, aged 15, support for Mary had grown and she became Queen.

For her aggressive actions during her pursuit of restoring Roman Catholicism in England and Ireland, history would dub her Bloody Mary. Ridley was sent to the Tower of London for his support for Lady Jane and his religious stance, along with many others who showed their support. Throughout February 1554, Jane and her political leaders were executed. Ridley was tried shortly after, being sentenced to burn at the stake. The sentence was carried out in October 1555 in Oxford, near what is now Broad Street, in front of a large crowd.

Facing the flames alongside him was Hugh Latimer, the Church of England Chaplain to Edward VI. Latimer is quoted as saying to Ridley,

'Be of good comfort, and play the man, Master Ridley; we shall this day light such a candle, by God's grace, in England, as I trust shall never be put out.' This quote is featured in Ray Bradbury's famous novel *Fahrenheit 451*. In remembrance a small metal cross marks the area this is believed to have taken place in Broad Street, with Ridley and Latimer being remembered as martyrs for their support of a Church of England independent from the Roman Catholic Church.

BURGLARY GONE WRONG

In winter 1907 staff in the North Eastern Co-Op branch in Windy Nook, Gateshead, began to notice goods going missing from their store during the night. With no signs of forced entry, they began to believe it was an inside job and, not wanting to tarnish the good name of the store, they set about creating a plan to capture the culprit. On the night of 1 November, three committee men and an apprentice lay waiting in the darkness hoping to catch the thief.

Sure enough, a man with a beard entered the shop with a lamp, looking to plunder some goods but completely unaware of the audience watching him. The men who watched in secret were John Patterson, Christopher Carr, John Joseph Cowell and George Ather. At around 10 p.m., the men gathered and it was not long before their plan sprang into action and an attempt to restrain the intruder began. Worried that he was taking too severe a beating, they allowed the man brief respite only for him to draw a revolver and shoot Mr Patterson in the head at point-blank range. Determined to escape, the thief then fired at Mr Carr, hitting him in the hip and leaving him permanently disabled. The remaining watchers tried to block the exits, but the burglar escaped via a window.

It was another three days before the perpetrator would be caught and during that time Mr Patterson died from his wound. The suspect was named Joseph William Noble, a local blacksmith, who the committee agreed could not have been the man in the shop as the intruder was a stranger. When police searched his house they found a number of goods from the Co-Op, a set of skeleton keys and the same type of lamp used in the burglary. Witnesses in court would later testify to having seen Noble in a fake beard during the months before, suggesting he had worn a disguise at the time.

This cautionary tale of taking justice into your own hands shocked the country and was reported nationwide. As with many well-publicised cases, crowds gathered when there was an opportunity to see the murderer in person, such as during his transportation to the courthouse. The marks he received from the struggle inside the butchers as well as the mountain of evidence against him would see him found guilty of murder and sentenced to hang. Protesting his innocence to the very end, Noble was executed in Durham on 24 March 1908 at the age of 48, with some of his last words being, 'Don't hurt my neck.'

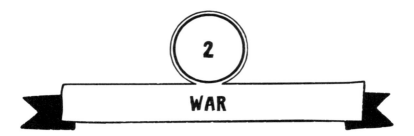

2

WAR

Since the days of Kane and Abel, brother has turned against brother, resulting in bloodshed. Far be it from me to romanticise the brutality of war, however, it is here, in the most extreme of situations, that people can be capable of incredible feats of strength and bravery that are worth commemorating in these tales.

A LUCKY ESCAPE FROM THE FRENCH REVOLUTION

The family of Thomas Gillow was one noted for its staunch loyalty to the Catholic faith. Born in Singleton, Lancashire, in 1769, after spending a few years at school Thomas travelled to France to study at the English college in Douai. It was during his stay here that the French Revolution broke out, jeopardising the lives of the students at the college.

Initially the college claimed exemption from revolutionary legislation due to the fact that it was English; however, as the revolution gained traction so did the pressure upon it. In 1791 the college printer was lynched by a mob and hanged from a lamp post after being accused of being 'obnoxious to the orators by the loyal tone of the press'. As more and more heads were fed to the guillotine across France, soldiers began knocking at the college door and soon most of its pupils fled back to

England. Gillow, alongside his friend Dr Penewick, made their escape from the country now in turmoil.

Upon arriving back in England, Gillow finished his theological studies at Crook Hall in Durham before eventually being appointed to North Shields. As the first rector of the now demolished St Cuthbert's Roman Catholic Church he is thought to have received over a thousand converts, becoming an immensely popular figure.

He remained in North Shields for thirty-six years, passing away in 1857 at the age of 88. His tomb, along with that of his nephew, Canon Richard Gillow, was said to be just outside the church. The first purpose-built Roman Catholic church outside Newcastle, St Cuthbert's was constructed in 1815 and was situated between Bedford Street and Albion Road prior to its demolition in the 1970s.

TAPPING THE ADMIRAL

The recipe for most people's ideal drink does not include a human corpse. Yet for some, drinking from a barrel containing a deceased hero was not a step too far. On the following pages, we will investigate some of the details surrounding the history of the phrase 'tapping the admiral' and its grim origin.

THE BATTLE OF TRAFALGAR

The phrase 'tapping the admiral' originates from a piece of folklore surrounding the death of Horatio Nelson at the Battle of Trafalgar in October 1805. The infamous battle, which took place during the Napoleonic Wars, is a piece of history kept in the minds of the public today by numerous monuments commemorating the heroic and brutal encounter. The Spanish and French naval fleets had combined their forces, clashing with the British Navy at sea, and ultimately leading to the death of Vice Admiral Horatio Nelson and defeat for Napoleon Bonaparte. Having been mortally wounded by a musket ball to his

TAPPING THE ADMIRAL

spine, Nelson died, just as victory appeared on the horizon – leaving the difficult question of how to transport his body back to his home country as per his request, rather than bury him at sea as was the norm.

The body was put into a casket and filled with alcohol by the ship's surgeon, William Beatty. It is widely accepted that the drink of choice was brandy mixed with camphor and myrrh, though some dispute this, believing it to be rum. His ship, *Victory*, was towed to Gibraltar before making its way back to England. While the use of alcohol was successful in preserving the body, it did not stop the decomposition process completely. One little-known anecdote relating to Nelson's journey home was that the gases produced by his rotting body had built up in the barrel he was kept in. Two weeks into the journey, the cask burst open, scaring the life out of the watchman on duty, who believed Nelson had returned from his eternal slumber and was attempting to get out.

TAPPING THE CASK

An article published in April 1933 in the *Sunderland Echo* tells of horrific consequences suffered by one sailor who partook in tapping the admiral. The article, which commemorates the sailor who passed away in 1852, tells how he was on board the ship with Nelson's body on his return voyage home. While attempting to spill the cask and drink the liquor, it tilted, crushing three of his knuckles and leaving them permanently dislocated. While some argue that 'tapping the admiral' originates from a toast in Nelson's honour, this sailor's tall tale offers another origin.

The story of the corpse in the cask has been told in many different settings and time periods around the world. One such story, which is alleged to have taken place shortly after the death of Nelson, is connected to another British military figure named General Edward Pakenham, who perished at the Battle of New Orleans in 1815. Legend has it that when transporting his body to Ireland in a casket of rum, he was accidentally diverted to South Carolina and delivered to a party – a mistake said to have not been realised until the drink was served.

American folklorist Jan Harold Brunvand documents an interesting version of the story in his book *The Choking Doberman* (2003, p.117), which he received from a professor of psychology at the University of South Dakota:

> Cheap bulk wine is imported from Algeria in ships, either arriving in Marseilles or by barge direct to Paris. The story always involves the slow draining of the tank into a bottling line, the departure of the bottles, and then the discovery at the bottom of the tank, too late to recall the bottles, of a dead Algerian. In one version the Algerian has a knife in his back; in another he has been strangled or hanged and still has the rope around his neck.

SUCKING THE MONKEY

The phrase 'sucking the monkey' is often considered an alternative for tapping the admiral and also has its roots in some grim history. When shipping monkeys from Africa to museums in the US and Great Britain, also during the nineteenth century, the same process was used to pickle the body for transportation. Folklorist William Neville Scott records a version of this story in his book *Pelicans Chihuahuas and Other Urban Legends* (1996, p.48) set once again in France:

> During the winter of 1861, the conductor of a train received for transport a huge parcel addressed to a professor of the College of France. It had been sent from Java. On the way to Paris, the train was held up on a siding waiting for an express to pass, and during the wait, the conductor and his assistant noticed the parcel was leaking. As the story puts it, it trickled '... *un liquide ambre, de gout tres fine at tres particulier.*' Naturally, he called in his mates, including the driver and fireman, and they boozed on until the express had passed. Wiping their moustaches, they hurriedly went on to their destination to be greeted by the professor, who informed them that the parcel held the body of a 'great ape of Borneo'.

THE BATTLE OF BOLDON HILL

While many of the stories in this chapter tell of heroism of natives and settlers from the North East doing their duty in different parts of the world, the Battle of Boldon Hill is one such event that took place here on our own soil.

During the first English Civil War battle lines were drawn all over Great Britain between Royalists and Parliamentarians. One such skirmish took place close to home when Parliamentarians, with assistance from Scottish Covenanters, marched across Northumberland and eventually ended up in Newcastle, which was seen as a Royalist stronghold.

Having had fair warning, those inside had time to fortify their walls and prepare for an attack. The Parliamentarians decided to continue further south to Sunderland and Durham but made a stop along the way. The Royalist forces went after their would-be attackers and on the journey the two forces became aware of each other's presence. The Royalists secured a position atop Boldon Hill, while the Parliamentarians gathered on Cleadon Hills, 3 miles away.

The day-long battle between the two armies would see a barrage of cannon fire, along with musket balls whizzing through the long grass. Eventually both parties retreated to their respective camps and hills. While neither party could really declare themselves the victor, the Royalist forces claimed to have killed or captured 1,000 Scots while admitting to a loss of 240 common soldiers, whereas the Scots claimed to have killed 1,500 Royalists while only admitting sixty killed and 300 wounded.

While war in England, let alone in Boldon, may seem like an impossibility these days, the remnants of invaders and conflicts on our soil continue to be found. It begs the question, are there any ghosts of the Battle of Boldon Hill still buried deep under the soil there?

RORKE'S DRIFT

In the South African province of Natal a battle took place that stands out in British history alongside the likes of Waterloo and Trafalgar.

Portrayed in the 1964 film *Zulu*, a defensive battle took place in which around 150 British troops stood their ground against 4,000 Zulu warriors in what is known as the Battle of Rorke's Drift.

The Zulu attack on the mission station at Rorke's Drift on 22 and 23 January 1879 came eleven days after the British invasion of Zululand and followed a defeat of Empire forces at the Battle of Islandlwana.

One soldier, Corporal William Wilson Allen, is reported to have been born in Newcastle, although there is debate around whether this was actually in a Northumbrian village. During the raging battle, the Zulu forces managed to gain entry to the field hospital in the mission and set it ablaze with many soldiers still inside.

Corporal Allen was said to have been one of the brave soldiers who held his post in a dangerous position, allowing the removal of the sick and injured men now trapped in the inferno.

Wave after wave of fighters battered the small collection of men desperately trying to hold onto their position, bayonet clashing against spear, until enough attacks had been repelled that the Zulu warriors retreated. The battle saw eleven Victoria Crosses awarded to soldiers, including Corporal Allen.

HANGING A MONKEY

This piece of folklore is something many of you in the North East may be familiar with but for those who are not it is worth hearing. In a colloquial jest, the people of Hartlepool have sometimes been referred to as monkey hangers, but where did this come from?

The story goes that during the Napoleonic Wars at the beginning of the 1800s a terrible storm wrecked a French vessel off the coast of Hartlepool. The wrecking of the ship claimed the lives of all their crew except one: a monkey dressed in a French army uniform that was thought to provide amusement for the crew. Upon discovering the hairy sailor on the beach, the locals arrested him and held a trial. With people not having seen a monkey nor a Frenchman before it was assumed he was a French spy, and as the poor primate was unable to defend himself he was sentenced to death by hanging.

Another theory is that a young boy who worked on the ship in the role of powder monkey, someone who primed cannon for fire using gunpowder, was actually the one hanged and not a literal monkey ... although I know which story I prefer.

DISTINGUISHED SERVICE

What does it take to be awarded a medal for distinguished service? Incredible bravery, if this story is anything to go by. Whilst serving in the Royal Navy during the First World War, Chief Petty Officer Henderson Miller Hellens showed such an attribute.

Only 17 at the time, he was aboard the ship when it encountered a sea mine. While likely not an uncommon occurrence, this would have been cause for alarm and in hushed voices a discussion on the best course of action would have played out. Our recipient then decided he would plunge into the water with a rope tied around his waist. Swimming up to the mine, heart racing, he pushed the mine to a distance clear of the ship, putting his own life in mortal danger to save the lives of his fellow crewmen.

The danger in this situation was very real and the resulting explosion injured Mr Hellens so badly that he had to stay in hospital for sixteen weeks. He received the DSM (Distinguished Service Medal) and returned to his life in Sunderland, where he worked as a boilerman at the Royal Infirmary.

Mr Henderson Miller Hellens passed away in 1977 and is buried in Bishopwearmouth Cemetery.

THE MURDER OF BISHOP WILLIAM WALCHER

After the Norman Conquest the north of England proved difficult to control. The border with Scotland having not yet been defined,

Saxon nobles used the area to carry out offensives against the invading Normans. The Saxons of the North East were frequently persecuted as a warning to any other unruly persons.

Liulph, who was an ancestor of the Lumley family of Lumley Castle, was on good terms with Bishop Walcher, who was Bishop of County Durham at the time. By having Liulph on his council he had a link to the local aristocracy and ally. However, when Walcher failed to act on an invasion by the Scottish leader Malcom III, Liulph criticised the bishop, who had allowed the North East to be ravaged for three weeks before the Scots left with slaves and plunder.

This feud between two of the most powerful men in the North East would result in both of their deaths. Walcher's men crept into the nobleman's hall in the middle of the night and murdered most of the household. The Northumbrians were enraged at having had one of their leaders murdered in cold blood and a genuine threat of rebellion arose.

Bishop Walcher came to realise this and in an attempt to calm the tension agreed to meet Liulph's kinsmen at Gateshead. He travelled with at least 100 men for protection to meet Eadulf Rus, the leader of the group. When he arrived he was presented with a petition of the wrongs committed, which he made the unfortunate decision to reject.

This caused an uproar and the enraged Northumbrians attacked the bishop's party, slaughtering many of his men. The bishop and what was left of his entourage fled into a nearby church, which was then set alight. As the building burned, the men, including Bishop Walcher, fled outside only to be cut down by the angry mob.

Following the killing of Walcher in 1080, the rebels attacked Walcher's castle at Durham and besieged it for four days, before returning to their homes. Their rising, and the killing of William the Conqueror's appointed bishop, led William to send his half-brother, Odo of Bayeux, with an army to harry the Northumbrian countryside. Many of the native nobility were driven into exile and the power of the Anglo-Saxon nobility in Northumbria was broken.

ONE OF THE FOUR HORSEMEN

In 1317 a terrible famine ravished Europe, spreading all over England including to the North East. Crop failures and death of livestock would see many turn to desperate acts to survive.

This quote from the *Historical Account of Newcastle-Upon-Tyne Including the Borough of Gateshead* by Eneas Mackenzie sheds a little light on the terrible scenes that occurred up here during this period:

> In 1317, there was a grievous famine and mortality at Newcastle, insomuch that the quick could hardly bury the dead, and a great corruption of cattle and grass. Some eat the flesh of their own children; and thieves in prison devoured those that were newly brought in, and greedily eat them half alive.

While not in modern vernacular, this account certainly paints vivid pictures of the horrors of what it was like to live in the North East at the time.

SIR HENRY HAVELOCK

Born in Ford Hall, Sunderland, on 5 April 1795, the son of a wealthy shipbuilder, Sir Henry Havelock and all his brothers entered careers in the army. Sir Henry fought in multiple wars in different countries but is particularly remembered for the role he played during the Indian Mutiny, which occurred during the British Imperial rule of India in 1857–59.

In 1857 a group of soldiers in the Bengal army shot their British officers and marched on Delhi. Rebellion broke out across vast swathes of the country and there were many casualties on both sides. Many of the civilian population took up arms, leaving many of the British who could not escape trapped and outnumbered.

Sir Henry had spent much time studying historic military strategies and put his knowledge to good use. He is remembered for the relief he provided to those besieged at Cawnpore and Lucknow, where he became trapped himself after more rebel forces arrived. He died of dysentery in Lucknow in November 1857, a few days after the siege was lifted.

Statues stand in Trafalgar Square, London, and Mowbray Park, Sunderland, in remembrance of him.

THE KOREAN WAR

While I think it is fair to say that most people in the UK, and indeed the North East, are familiar with the dictator Kim Jong-un and his late father, Kim Jong-il, I doubt many of us could explain how the Democratic Republic of Korea, or North Korea as it is commonly known, came to be.

Korea was ruled by Imperial Japan after being annexed in 1910, until the end of the Second World War when Japan surrendered. Much like Germany, Korea was split into two zones of administration: one under the Soviet Union and the other under the United States. As Cold War tensions increased, the two became sovereign states, one socialist the other capitalist, with both leaders claiming to be the sole leader of a unified Korea.

In 1950 North Korean forces made a move on the South, sending its forces over territorial lines. This led the United Nations to dispatch South Korean forces and lend additional military support. While 90 per cent of this came from the United States, some of the international peacekeeping force came from the UK.

When UN troops began closing in on the Chinese border with the aim of unifying Korea under a pro-Western government, China became involved. Included in the 100,000 or so British troops involved in the fighting were the North East regiment the Northumberland Fusiliers, who were stationed in north-west Korea.

In one clash against Communist forces in December 1950, a three-day-long battle resulted in five British casualties, whereas the enemy force suffered 300. In a message from a commanding officer of the US

First Corps, Lieutenant General Frank Milburn, to the 29th Brigade, the following was said of the incident:

> The action of your brigade was magnificent and has proved a source of inspiration. The brigade held against overwhelming numbers. British courage and skill and willingness to stand the test have never been more widespread than on this occasion.

After much fighting, a stalemate would eventually come to be reached, and soon after a demilitarised zone was set up in 1953 with both sides withdrawing from their fighting positions. The two countries are technically still at war and the border between them is thought to be the most fortified in the world today.

THE BIRTLEY BELGIANS

When the First World War began the British Government realised that its current rate of production for national armaments would not cover the necessary demand for shells to defeat the German Imperial Army. To help remedy this, new factories were commissioned across the country and Belgians, renowned for their excellent armament factories, were brought over to help staff them.

In 1915, Elizabethville was created in the northern edge of Birtley, Gateshead, so that wounded soldiers and refugees could work in the huge armaments factory. The colony was seen as Belgian sovereign ground and it operated according to that country's law, with restricted access to the public. The enclave grew to a population of approximately 6,000 and housed its own hospital, schools and church with hostels for single men and cottages for families.

On 20 December 1916 a confrontation occurred when a worker went to speak to the military head of security to request a few days' leave. The worker was not wearing full regulation uniform as required under Belgian law and was sent to a cell for four days as punishment. This immediately riled the other workers, who saw this as unjust, and a crowd 2,000 strong almost broke into a riot. The military head of security was replaced and the worker set free to resolve the situation.

The Armistice in 1918 put a sudden end to the enterprise and the Belgians were quickly repatriated. The Birtley Belgians were said to have produced shells superior to any other in the land and even most of Europe. Elizabethville quickly became a ghost town with many of the buildings being taken over by the poor and homeless. In the 1930s almost all the village was destroyed to make way for new housing and only two buildings survive to this day, which are the old food store and butchers.

ZEPPELIN RAID — SUNDERLAND, 1916

On the morning of 1 April 1916, Zeppelin L110 left its airbase in Nordholz, Germany, on a mission to target the industry in Sunderland and surrounding areas. While Zeppelins may appear to have been large and slow, at the time they were very difficult to shoot down as they could climb higher than many aircraft, and while holes could be shot in them this alone would not be enough to take them down.

The Zeppelin arrived at approximately 10 p.m., blocking out the skies as it floated over Sunderland. Twenty bombs were dropped from the gondola suspended from the aircraft, killing twenty people and injuring over 100. The bombs wreaked havoc on the area, destroying houses, disrupting roads and doing damage to much of the local industry. The Zeppelin came under fire from anti-aircraft guns at Fulwell, then went on to attack targets in Middlesbrough before returning back to its base.

As a result of this attack, an acoustic mirror was built in 1917 to help detect German airships. The device reflected sound into the microphone, which would give the operator a fifteen-minute warning of an incoming attack. The acoustic mirror is one of the last remaining in the UK and was recently restored in 2015 and is located near Fulwell Windmill.

ZEPPELIN RAID

THE FIRST SHOT FIRED

John Lindsay McCutcheon Brown-King was born on 10 June 1890 in Sherriff Hill, Gateshead. The fourth of what would be five sons, John's parents were Frederick Brown-King, who was a coal miner, and Jane Hamilton McCutcheon, who was the daughter of a colliery engineman. It is largely accepted that John was the first person to fire a shot in the First World War for Britain while engaging the German minelayer *Königen Luise* at sea.

In 1901, John is recorded as living at home with his family at Carr's Hill Lodge in Gateshead. Seven years later he enlisted with the Royal Marines Light Infantry at the age of 17. When the First World War broke out in 1914, John was on board HMS *Amphion* as a gun layer. The ship was patrolling the North Sea when a report from a trawler that had seen a ship throwing things overboard reached the small fleet of which *Amphion* was a member. It was correctly assumed the objects were mines and the fleet spread out in search of the ship, locating it quickly.

The war had officially begun less than thirty-two hours prior to this encounter but this first action would prove to be deadly. John is reported to have fired the first shot from the *Amphion* and went on to sink *Königen Luise*, taking down the German flag. The ship eventually sank and the crew were distributed among the small fleet as prisoners. This victory was short lived, however, as soon after the *Amphion* collided with one of the mines laid by *Königen Luise*. John was severely injured while attempting to rescue a fellow soldier but he did make it off the ship alive. The incident claimed the lives of over 100 people, some of which were prisoners taken from the German ship that laid the mines.

John was taken to Shotley hospital to recover and both his parents travelled down to visit him. He succumbed to his injuries seventeen days later, on 23 August 1914. His father informed people how well the injured were taken care of in the hospital at the time and also relayed some of John's final words in a letter published in the *Newcastle Journal*. This extract is taken from the letter:

They have damaged me, but I have damaged them, too. Never mind, mother, I have had the pleasure and great honour of knocking the German flag down. I fetched it with my second shot, and I fetched the mast level with the deck with my third shot. I fired fourteen shots and I had seven hits. That was not bad for a start.

John is buried in Shotley Churchyard near Harwich in Suffolk. An individual plaque is also dedicated to him in St Alban's Church in Windy Nook, Gateshead. He was awarded the 1914 Star, the British War Medal and the Victory Medal for his service. Over 700 men from the small parish of Windy Nook answered the call, many giving their life for the freedoms we enjoy today.

CRIMEAN WAR VETERANS

The Crimean War erupted in 1853 and lasted until 1856. While the reasons behind the conflict are complex, religious rights and international politics were the main causes, as is usually the case with events such as this. Primarily fought between the Russian Federation and an alliance of the Ottoman Empire, France, Britain and Sardinia, the chaos of those three years saw many butchered from all over the globe. The Crimean War is also considered one of the first conflicts to use modern technology such as exploding naval shells, railways and telegraphs. In this story I will not go into much detail of the specifics of the war as there is too much information to cover, but will instead touch on some of the North East men who fought bravely on behalf of their country there.

George James Nightingale was a Blyth resident who first entered naval service as a second-class boy before seeing action in the Crimean War. He served for thirty-five years in the Queen's Navy as well as working as a member of the Coastguard for a number of years. He died aged 66 in 1900 and is buried in Blyth Cemetery.

Corporal John Cooper was a South Shields native who fought in the battles of Alma, Inkerman and Sevastopol. Cooper was among the first troops to land in Crimea following the outbreak of war. He died aged 83 in 1908 at his daughter's home in South Shields and his funeral was attended by a large crowd, many of whom were other North East veterans.

Cornelius Cronnin from Sunderland was drafted to fight in the Crimean War in 1854. He was awarded the Crimean Medal as well as clasps for the Sevastopol, Alma, Inkerman and Balaklava battles. He also served under Sir Henry Havelock during the Indian Mutiny, where he also received a medal for his services at Lucknow. At the time of his death in 1895 he was 65 and is reported to have been held in high esteem by the people in the community of Monkwearmouth where he lived.

William Fitzgerald was born in Ireland in 1832 and joined the military aged 18. His service in Crimea saw him receive the Turkish Medal as well as a number of other decorations. He also saw service in India and China, serving over twenty-one years in the military, before he eventually moved to Gateshead and settled down, working at the Gateshead Dispensary. He passed away in 1914, aged 82, at his home in Gateshead.

James Sly was a North Shields resident and Crimean War veteran who fell on hard times after his service. He was reported as being a member of the old Black Watch and as he got older he was looked after by the North Shields and District Veterans Association, who purchased a small home for him. James passed away aged 82 in 1915 and is buried in Preston Cemetery.

These men are only a handful of those who witnessed the conflict in Crimea. Online there are numerous records of brave men from the North who travelled overseas for Queen and country to follow orders, likely looking for adventure and glory, but often finding only violence and death. The war ended in 1856 after the allies gained more support and Russia sued for peace, signing the Treaty of Paris.

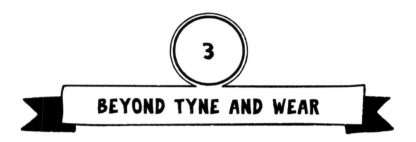

BEYOND TYNE AND WEAR

Some of my favourite tales in this eclectic collection take place outside Tyne and Wear. Many a strange thing has happened in our little corner of the earth, and by delving into some of the more bizarre and unusual episodes in this chapter I hope you are encouraged to venture beyond the border and explore more of the North East.

It's not just coal mines and ships up here yanar.

REINCARNATION

Joanna Pollock was the first daughter born to Florence and John Pollock in 1946 before the family moved to Hexham, Northumberland, a couple of years later. In 1951 their second daughter, Jacqueline, was born and the two were said to be inseparable. Although he grew up in a Christian background, John Pollock was a firm believer in reincarnation, unlike his wife, and is reported to have often prayed for evidence of its proof.

In 1957 tragedy struck while the girls were walking to church one morning and they were hit by a car, which killed them instantly. Their parents were understandably devastated; however, John remained hopeful that one day the daughters would be reborn again into the family. Florence did fall pregnant again this time, with twins despite there not being any known history of this in either family. In 1958

Florence gave birth to two little girls the couple named Gillian and Jennifer, and to this day they are believed by some to be proof of reincarnation.

The girls were identical, although Jennifer had birthmarks that some pointed to as partial proof of this argument. Jennifer had a mark on her face in the same place that Jacqueline had a scar at a young age, and they also shared a birthmark in the same place. The girls were said to possess knowledge of things they could not have possibly know about, such as details of the accident and information on toys that had belonged to their dead sisters. The family had moved from Hexham when the girls were just 9 months old, however when they returned four years later they are reported to have known the way to the park and the schools.

The strange statements made by the girls and the seemingly unknowable knowledge they possessed made them one of the most famous claimed cases of reincarnation in British history. However, some argue that because of John's firm belief in reincarnation prior to these events it is likely that he talked about some of these details in front of the children.

RUTH FIRST

Ruth First was born in South Africa to Jewish parents Julius First and Matilda Levetan, who arrived in the country from Latvia in the early 1900s. They became founding members of the South African Communist Party prior to Ruth's birth in 1925, and it seemed the stage would be set for a child with a destiny in political activism.

Growing up in Johannesburg, there is no doubt that Ruth bore witness to the horrors of apartheid, which would have influenced her following in her parents' footsteps by joining the Communist Party, which was allied with the African National Congress (ANC).

She was the first woman in her family to attend university and became involved in student activism, meeting figures who would become infamous in South Africa such as Nelson Mandela. Over the years her passion for ending apartheid grew, leading her to take part in protests in the 1950s that saw further tightening of laws and restriction of movement.

Her determination would see her put on trial for treason, with her academic work being used as evidence to support the charge. Although she would ultimately be acquitted, she would later be imprisoned and put in isolation for 117 days in 1963 during another government crackdown. This led her to leave the country and live in exile.

Ruth came to London in March 1964 and got involved in the British anti-apartheid movement, rallying support for her cause back home. She began lecturing and found herself up in the North East teaching Development Studies at the University of Durham between 1973 and 1978.

Her love for her country would eventually see her return to the African continent. This time she took the role of director of research at the Centre of African Studies at the Universidade Eduardo Mondlane in Maputo in Mozambique, a role that would sadly be her last. While employed there she opened a parcel bomb that put an abrupt end to her life. The assassination was carried out to silence her on the orders of a Major in the South African Police Force.

Ruth's legacy is still felt globally and in the North East. The University of Durham still has the Ruth First Educational Trust, which provides opportunities for students from southern Africa to undertake postgraduate study at Durham University. In 2022 a mural was restored and unveiled on Providence Row, Durham, celebrating Ruth and her connection to the city forty years after her assassination.

BIG BUG

Much like a scene from the iconic film *Starship Troopers*, there was a time when big bugs roamed the Earth. When you think of fossil finds from millions of years ago places like the Jurassic Coast in Dorset spring to mind, but one amazing find off the Northumberland coast may change that.

The fossil of a giant millipede-like specimen, called Arthropleura, was discovered inside a large block of sandstone on the beach at Howick Bay. Over 326 million years ago, when this creature was alive, the North East of England's climate was much more tropical than the chilly weather we have today.

The creature was discovered by a PhD student by accident while walking along the beach and is only the third such find of its kind in existence as well as being recognised as the oldest and largest.

Thought to have been found in what was once an old river channel, the fossil is the exoskeleton that the beast shed as it grew. While little is known of the creature's habits, it is theorised that its diet consisted of nuts and seeds supplemented by other small creatures and amphibians.

Dating from the Carboniferous Period, 100 million years before dinosaurs, it becomes obvious why fossils of this kind are so rare. While there are others in existence, a head of one of these giant bugs is yet to be discovered. Could this be hiding in the rocks of some North East coastline?

A WOLF IN THE WILD

The presence of native wolves in Great Britain dates back to early Roman and Saxon times, when their population was said to flourish. Due to the risk they posed to livestock and human life, the wolf was hunted to extinction and by the reign of Henry VII (1485–1509) there were thought to be few or no wolves left in England.

In October 1904 a wolf belonging to Captain Barnes of Shotley Bridge, County Durham, escaped into the wilds of the North East. Reports soon began to surface of farmers waking up in the morning to find their sheep slaughtered and the story soon caught the attention of the newspapers. The wolf made its way towards Allendale, where it made further kills and was seen near Allenhead School.

Panic soon gripped the people of Northumberland as farmers began keeping their animals indoors at night and groups got together to search the woods. A bounty was placed on the animal and the Hexham Wolf Committee was formed to track it down. Sightings continued

A WOLF IN THE WILD

throughout December and the elusive predator even managed to avoid renowned game hunters and bloodhounds.

On 29 December the carcass of an animal killed by a passing train was discovered near Cumwinton. The body was not initially thought to be that of a wolf and was buried, but after discussing it with the stationmaster it was dug up again and brought to the Wolf Committee for identification. Captain Barnes declared the wolf too old to be his and that the real wolf must still be at large, but by the end of January 1905 interest dwindled until finally stories about it disappeared altogether.

THE GUNPOWDER PLOT

Guy Fawkes's infamous plot to blow up the House of Lords with gunpowder is a part of British history that is commemorated every year on 5 November. His plan to kill King James I and most of the entire ruling class was not to be carried out alone, however, and one member of their group was a man from the North East.

Born around 1563, Thomas Percy was one of the core members involved in the plot. While little is said to be known about the early years of his life, Percy converted to Catholicism and was also appointed constable of Alnwick Castle by his second cousin once removed, Henry Percy, 9th Earl of Northumberland, making him responsible for the Percy family's northern estates. When King James I ascended to the throne in 1603, Percy was not pleased as he believed the new King had gone back on promises he had made about tolerance for English Catholics. Robert Catesby was another man who was not happy with the new monarch and after they had a meeting in June 1603 he joined the conspiracy to kill the King.

Percy was a key part of the gunpowder plot as he helped fund the group as well as secure leases to certain properties in London, including the undercroft directly beneath the House of Lords in which the gunpowder was finally placed. The plot was foiled on 5 November 1605 after a midnight search uncovered Guy Fawkes guarding thirty-five barrels of gunpowder. The plot was in part exposed due to a letter, believed by some to have been written by Thomas Percy, warning one of the Lords not to attend, which prompted the thorough search. Fawkes was arrested immediately and it was Percy's name that appeared on the first arrest warrant.

The northern plotter had been warned of Fawkes's capture, giving him enough time to escape immediate punishment. Fellow conspirator Christopher Wright fled alongside him, meeting Catesby and the others in the Midlands. His daring escape did not last long, however, as only two days later, on 7 November, Percy and Catesby were besieged at Holbeche House near the Staffordshire border. Percy was killed alongside his fellow conspirator in the firefight that ensued and was later buried nearby. Unfortunately his body did not rest there, as under the orders of the Earl of Northampton, both corpses were exhumed and their heads displayed on pikes outside the Houses of Parliament.

While some of those involved in the conspiracy suffered the gruesome fate of being hung, drawn and quartered, Guy Fawkes did not. Rather than be subjected to this painful death, he jumped from the gallows and broke his own neck, so as not to give those who wanted to punish him the satisfaction.

WILD, WILD NORTHUMBERLAND

Andrew Young was born in 1927 in Northumberland. His father was a mining engineer who had spent many years living in India, which is where Young attended Bishop Cotton School in Shimla. With the outbreak of the Second World War, he was drafted in as a British Army intelligence officer in Austria tasked with locating and arresting war criminals. After his return to England he studied architecture in Newcastle and Durham before marrying and moving to Australia.

While in Australia he found work as an architect and participated in the design of the Australia Square building in Sydney in 1964. His skills saw him work in the Middle East, Africa, India, Canada, Central America and the UK. In the 1970s Andrew left his career and went travelling, eventually arriving back in India, this time in Pune, where he took sannyasi becoming a follower of Bhagwan Shree Rajneesh. It was here he worked in the kitchen and as a handyman in the boutique until 1981.

Eventually he travelled to Rajneeshpuram, a city built in Oregon in the US by followers of Bhagwan, where his skills were utilised in the architect's office. Dealing directly with Ma Anand Sheela, Bhagwan's right-hand follower, he went on to marry Shavda, who ran the Rajneesh hotel in Portland for a time. The controversial city clashed with residents of the nearby town of Antelope, escalating with a select group of followers committing the largest bioterrorism attack on American soil in its history. Rajneeshpuram would eventually be shut down after numerous disputes, internal fighting and further controversy following the confirmation of bioterrorism.

Following the closure of Rajneeshpuram, Andrew and Shavda travelled before settling in San Diego, California, with friends from the ranch in Oregon. In 1989 he moved to Guatemala, following Shavda, where he established a commune in Santa Cruz called La Iguana Perdida. It is here that Andrew retired before passing away aged 90. Known to some as Prem Sarito, the name given to him by Bhagwan Shree Rajneesh, and Andrew to others, his life was one that can be said to have been extraordinary. For those interested in more information on Rajneeshpuram, I thoroughly recommend giving the documentary *Wild Wild Country*, available on Netflix, a watch.

Did you know that Gateshead used to be home to Europe's largest indoor theme park? Metroland, tucked away in the Metrocentre, will be a fond memory for those who had the chance to visit but has long since disappeared.

THE DISAPPEARANCE OF DARWIN

This is a story that captured the attention not only of us locals up here in the North East but nationally. A tale that is perhaps more suitable to the 1800s, in which a death is faked and a man lives in hiding.

John Darwin was born in Hartlepool, County Durham, in August 1950. Trying his hand at a number of jobs over the years, he first became a teacher before becoming a prison officer as well as being a landlord.

In 2002, Darwin paddled his kayak out into the frosty March sea at Seaton Carew by himself, only to disappear amongst the waves. That same day he would be reported missing after failing to appear at his job, immediately setting alarm bells ringing. With his last-known whereabouts placing him in the sea, a large-scale search was launched with a large swathe of the coastline being covered in the hope of finding him.

No immediate trace of him was found except for a double-ended paddle, which was located in the sea near where it is thought he entered the waves. However, the day after he vanished his kayak was found in a damaged state. This left investigators baffled, as the sea was unusually calm at the time of his disappearance.

Darwin would ultimately be declared dead and his wife would go on to collect on his life insurance policy. All was not as it seemed, though, in the Darwin household and this would come to light five years later in 2007.

Darwin had not disappeared at all. In a cunning plan hatched between him and his wife, he had faked his death and had in fact been living in the house next door to the one in which his wife lived.

During the time in which he was presumed dead he didn't do the best job of maintaining his cover. Lee Wadrop, a tenant of one of the Darwin family's bedsits, would bump into him and recognise him. In a conversation fit for a comedy sketch, Lee asked: 'Aren't you supposed to be dead?'

To which Darwin replied, 'Don't tell anyone about this.'

Not wanting to get involved, Wadrop did not report the sighting to the police.

Darwin was even able to leave the country and return under a false passport with the name John Jones. At one point a work colleague of his wife, Anne Darwin, heard a phone conversation between the couple that raised alarm bells.

During the time Darwin had been living in secret, the couple had been investing in property in Panama. A change in visa laws would see him unable to continue with his investment plans without a verification process that he knew his false alias would not pass. Therefore he took the bold step of returning to the UK and embellishing his lie by feigning amnesia, which was the beginning of the end for him.

His tall tale unravelled and with evidence mounting against him the curtain was pulled back, revealing the truth of the whole affair.

In 2008 the couple were sentenced to more than six years in prison. This story was recently dramatised on ITV as *The Thief, His Wife and the Canoe* (2022).

THE CURSE OF THE DIRTY BOTTLES

Not far from Alnwick Castle lies the infamous pub known as Ye Olde Cross Inn. Perhaps one of the oldest watering holes in the region, as its history stretches back over two centuries, this relatively small building houses a well-known piece of interesting folklore.

Behind an aged window lies a collection of bottles that are said to have been untouched by human hands for over 200 years. The story goes that when a former landlord was putting the bottles in the window to display them he keeled over and died of a heart attack. Some versions of the story tell how he put a curse on the bottles as he lay dying, while in other versions it is his widow who promises that anyone who touches the bottles will follow the deceased landlord to the grave. As a result, the window was sealed and locked up tight to prevent any more fatalities that might occur from the cursed objects.

Interestingly, a report in the *Newcastle Chronicle* in 1960 tells how a landlord named Cyril Walker had spooky experiences after taking over the pub. As Cyril was a former police officer, it is probably fair to say he was not a man who was scared easily, but when things began moving in the night he was left puzzled. Beer mats are said to have been found stacked on top of each other and carpets moved from beneath tables, as well as the sounds of glass clinking in the night. Despite checking after hearing these noises, he found no intruder and no explanation.

Whether the curse of the dirty bottles is a clever way of pulling in the punters or something more sinister will for now remain a mystery. Either way, this is one story that has stood the test of time.

THE CURSE OF THE DIRTY BOTTLES

THE ALNWICK CASTLE VAMPIRE

Along the North East coast lies the ancient Alnwick Castle, which was finished around 1136, having been started after the Norman conquest of the region. The castle has been featured in a number of films but arguably the most interesting tale attached to it is an old one related to the blood-sucking undead.

While stories of vampires are traditionally more common in Eastern Europe than England, this one dates back to the twelfth century long before Bram Stoker would write *Dracula*. Archived by twelfth-century historian William Newburgh, who focused on stories of souls returning from the dead, he published this particular tale in his book *Historia Rerum Anglicarum*.

The story goes that the lord of the estate at the time had grown suspicious of his wife, suspecting her of having an adulterous relationship, and had hatched a plan to catch her in the act. While seated atop the castle to spy on her, he fell and suffered terrible injuries. His wife denied the affair, looking after him following the accident; however, his injuries proved fatal and he perished before having the chance to confess his sins. Due to the fact that the man died unrepentant, many believed he was cursed to walk the earth and strange things were said to have begun happening in the area.

The following night the man was reportedly spotted in the town, having come from the tunnels beneath the castle. Soon after a mysterious illness began plaguing the town, with locals blaming the deaths on the alleged creature of the night. One Palm Sunday a local priest, along with a mob, dug up the grave and reportedly found the body still very much filled with blood. Convinced the blame lay with the long-buried corpse, it was taken to town and burned. Interestingly, following this strange ritual the epidemic seemed to die down and rumours of the undead faded into history.

Recorded cases of the plague visiting Alnwick at this time may help explain the creation of this story as the townspeople no doubt feared for their lives. There are also believed to have been other historic cases connected to vampire mythology that are tied to Alnwick Castle, although evidence of this is scarce. There are many different versions of this story, and while I cannot vouch for its credibility, it certainly makes for an interesting piece of folklore from the North East.

Did you know that the UK is home to a number of volcanos? It may disappoint or relieve you to know none of these are active and were last such in the Paleogene period some 50 million years ago. One such volcano is in the North East in Northumberland and is named The Cheviot.

THE LAST BOAR

Since a time before recorded history, wild boar would roam the English countryside. Living in forested areas and among the untamed wild brush that would come to be replaced by office blocks and call centres, these native creatures would provide a food resource for locals for centuries.

Sadly, though, as is often the case, the expansion of the human race in conjunction with little to no understanding of conservationism would see this population dwindle to extinction.

Wild boar did have the potential to be deadly, though, when encountered in the wild, with large ivory tusks that could penetrate a man's flesh as if it were a rubber balloon. Roger de Ferry is recorded as having killed the last wild boar in County Durham in the 1200s in what is known as the slaying of the Brawn of Brancepeth.

Legend has it that knights far and wide travelled to make a name as the one to slay the Brawn of Brancepeth but the boar was too nimble and would elude its fate every time. De Ferry tracked the beast for an unknown length of time, studying its movements and routes, until one day the two would meet on a path favoured by the boar.

Drawing his sword, de Ferry clashed with the beast, bringing about its untimely end. Regarded as a hero by the locals at the time, the tale of Roger De Ferry and the beastly boar would cement his place in the annals of history, with the story first being recorded by renowned Durham historian Robert Surtees.

HAND OF GLORY

Superstition and folklore surrounding supernatural powers gained from the hands of dead men can be traced to different parts of the globe and span the centuries. One such early European belief was known as the Hand of Glory, which dates back to the 1600s when the severed hand of a hanged man would be mummified and dried out before fat and hair from the deceased would be used to make a candle with the hand.

It was believed that, when lit, the candle would provide the holder with supernatural powers, allowing them to be invisible and immobilising others in the household. These attributes made it especially desirable for thieves, who are often featured in stories of its use.

Perhaps the most famous story in English folklore to feature the Hand of Glory is set in 1797 at the Spital Inn, Stainmore, in Cumbria. Late at night an old woman knocks on the door of the inn requesting shelter for the evening and is welcomed in by the innkeeper. Once everyone has retired for the night, the maid notices that the weary old traveller is wearing men's clothes underneath her dress and feigns sleep so as to spy on the visitor. In the dead of the night the maid follows the old 'woman' into the kitchen, where he drops his disguise and pulls a Hand of Glory from a sack and proceeds to chant an incantation. The maid tries to wake the innkeeper but is unable to do so and instead extinguishes the candle's flame, breaking the spell and catching the thief. Another similar example of this story exists in Northumberland where the maid, after being unable to extinguish the flame with other means, pours a jug of milk over the candle and locks the house, trapping the thief inside.

One modern example featuring the Hand of Glory being used can be seen in *Harry Potter and the Chamber of Secrets*, when Draco Malfoy sees one in Borgin and Burkes, the dark arts specialist shop. The hand is then featured again later in *Harry Potter and the Half-Blood Prince* when Draco buys and uses it. The only known Hand of Glory to survive today was discovered in 1935 walled up inside a cottage in Castleton, and is currently housed in Whitby Museum.

> Let those who rest more deeply sleep,
> Let those awake their vigils keep,
> O Hand of Glory, shed thy light,
> Direct us to our spoil tonight.

HAND OF GLORY

THE WEIRD

Where would we be without the weird? Very bored I imagine.

Without getting too preachy on you, the world is a diverse tapestry woven with many a unique thread. Sure it can sometimes be funny to laugh at the strange or unusual but there is also a lot to be learned. What do you take for granted as normal but to plenty of others is probably a bit odd?

We all have a bit of the weird in us; embrace it, for it is what makes you you.

THE KING'S EVIL

What is the king's evil, you might ask? Some of you may have learned about this in school while others may not have heard of it, but I hope that none of you have indeed suffered from king's evil.

The king's evil, more commonly known in modern times as scrofula, a type of tuberculosis, would see its sufferers endure a variety of terrible symptoms that included chills, sweats, and fevers. Its victims' lymph nodes also swell, resulting in a distortion of their appearance and producing sores on the body.

With little understanding of disease, contagion or in fact healthcare, there was not a great deal to be done to help those who had contracted it. That is except enlist the touch of royalty!

Beginning in the sixteenth century, the practice of royalty, members of which were said to have inherited their gifts and wealth by divine right, would see monarchs lay their hands on those suffering with the aim of curing the affliction. While the process can trace its lore further into the past than Henry VII, he is thought to have been the first to legitimise it.

By a member of royalty laying their hands on the afflicted it is thought the process would rid the disease from the body. What is interesting, though is that the disease itself was rarely fatal and often went into remission on its own, leaving sufferers with the belief that the cure was delivered by royalty or the divine.

In June 1633, King Charles I entered Durham, where he was entertained at great expense by Bishop Morton. During his two-day stay the King laid his hands on those who had the king's evil, showing that even the people from the North East are not immune to a 'touch' of showmanship.

LIEUTENANT DARING

In an age before Netflix people would often leave their house and do activities in communal groups without a phone in their hand. Tough to believe, I know!

This meant that entertainment was more competitive, with fairs and theatres packed with diverse acts all competing for a bustling audience. Just like Daredevil Schreyer I wrote about in the first instalment of *Tyne and Weird*, Lieutenant Daring was another amateur stuntman looking to cash in on thronging crowds baying for the next exciting act.

Billy Welsby, also known as Lieutenant Daring, served in the First World War, where he became a lieutenant and won the medal of valour. After the war, however, he struggled with family issues and decided to take up touring on the entertainment circuit. On Sunderland Town Moor in June 1929 the lieutenant found his crowd. Having created a tower over 30ft tall, he made his way to the top and dived off into a shallow tank below before a stunned audience. It is also reported that later that night, to finish his act, the performer set himself alight!

The stuntman was not always so lucky, though, and when performing at a carnival at Willington in North Tyneside during August the same year he would suffer a tragic injury. This time he again climbed his tall tower with eyes locked on his every move and dived off into a 4ft-deep tank, a feat he called the 'death dive'.

This time he clipped the tank and bobbed face down in the water for some time before he was pulled out to safety. When taken to a nearby infirmary it was found he had a dislocated spine and he would wait weeks for a family member to organise for an ambulance to take him to Bolton General Hospital.

Lieutenant Daring would die two years later, meaning he made his last great performance up here in the North East.

LIFE AND DEATH IN THE NORTH EAST

Here is a story from the *Sunderland Herald* dating back to the 1800s of a journalist visiting an elderly couple in County Durham. Upon entering the old married couple's abode, the reporter found the couple engaged in a deep conversation. The wife was very ill, it seemed, and the couple were discussing the funeral arrangements that were to be made. The couple worked through their calculations, adding the costs of the coffin, plot and headstone until all was totalled up. The couple were not pleased with how much the grand total had come to and were grumbling, when the husband was struck with an idea.

'Well Janet lass ye may not die after all ye ken,' he exclaimed.

'Deed, and I hope not, Robert,' she replied.

'For I am quite sure we canna afford it,' was his response.

BRONZE AGE FIND

While researching many of these stories that point far back into the past, I often stumble across papers and articles that highlight the amazing discoveries of people who have built up our cities and streets from the

BRONZE AGE FIND

ground up. Although you can sometimes unearth forgotten tombs or relics from civilisations long gone, the number of these discoveries seem to be dwindling over time.

However, one recent discovery in Penshaw proves that the earth beneath our feet still holds many secrets to be shared, as a site earmarked for building new houses shows. While conducting an archaeological survey, a Bronze Age urn was uncovered, tying in with other finds in the Sunderland area.

The urn dates back to between 2100 and 750 BC and is believed to contain the remains of someone very important, perhaps even a potential ruler of the area. The era characterised by its prominent use of bronze saw the increase in individual burial rituals rather than communal. With that said, the area where the urn was uncovered also contains evidence of cremation pits nearby where the remains of those less important would have been burnt.

If, like me, you are keen on the odd horror movie, I am sure you will be all too familiar with what happens to those who build on top of graveyards …

SOMETHING FISHY

Here is a tale that goes back many years, to 20 June 1559. In the book *The History and Antiquities of the Town and County of the Town of Newcastle Upon Tyne: Including an Account of the Coal Trade of that Place* a marvellous story of lost property is told.

A Mr Anderson, merchant and alderman, was leaning over a bridge that ran over the River Tyne fiddling with a ring on his finger. To his horror, the ring slipped off, plunging into the icy waters below. No doubt understanding the impossible task of hunting out his jewellery, he accepted the card he had been dealt and moved on.

In a twist akin to that of a Hollywood movie, and even considered suspicious in the book in which it was recorded, his servant was at the market purchasing some food for his master. Deciding on salmon, he forked over his coin and returned to their home. The very same ring

SOMETHING FISHY

that was lost to his master appeared to have been swallowed by the fish that had been bought by his servant. In another book the ring is recorded as being in the possession of Rev. E. Anderson, of Yorkshire, and now has a fish engraved under the signet.

GHOST CAPTURED

In 1886 the people of Felling, Gateshead, were being plagued by the presence of a ghost who would creep up to houses, rattling their windows and doors as well as being seen lurking behind walls. This had been going on for six weeks, with the residents gradually growing frustrated at their elusive visitor from beyond the grave.

It seems the ghoul's luck ran out, though, as in January a man brandishing a poker gave chase, likely caught by surprise as he was only wearing a shirt, and was heard shouting, 'For God's sake stop that ghost.'

An angry mob soon formed and the ghost quickly fled into the police station. Unsurprisingly, the ghost turned out to be nothing more than a young man who was very thankful to have police protection.

Did you know that during the Covid-19 pandemic, Tyne and Wear museums collected archive material of this unusual time, a novel idea that future generations can look back on. One of the stranger things donated was hair grown by two men over the course of lockdown, presumably because they could not get to the barbers.

AN EVENTFUL WEDDING

While every wedding is a special occasion, sometimes these events can take a turn for the strange and sometimes worse.

One such example of this took place in Cleadon in June 1862, when coachman R. Shortridge was enjoying his marriage ceremonies with people from the village. A number of young men had loaded guns to celebrate by shooting into the sky. The son of a local farmer, jokingly we shall assume, pointed a gun at another villager and said aloud: 'I am going to shoot you.' Then George Swinhoe was struck in the neck, dying almost immediately, which turned the happy occasion into a tragic affair. George was only 18 years old and Thomas Stephenson, the young man who had pulled the trigger in jest , was said to be devastated, although he was ultimately arrested for the accidental crime.

Another tale of wedding woes describes how in Sunderland in 1853 the wedding of two gypsy families took place. During the celebrations it seems a riot broke out among the guests, which resulted in both the bride and groom being sent to the gaol to serve two months' each for assault.

Love does seem to know no rhyme or reason, as in October 1852 a keelman named Benjamin Lee from Blyth married Isabella Baxter. Both parties were 73 years of age and it was in fact the ninth time that Mrs Baxter had been married.

The final strange marriage listing I have come across tells how in April 1891 it is reported that a woman of 32 inches tall married a giant. With little more description available than that this happened in South Shields, I am sure you, the reader, can work out the rest.

LADY PEAT THE KLEPTOMANIAC

The lore of the eccentric has long since been one that fascinates me. When we see a homeless man or woman on the street carrying a lot of bags it is sometimes whispered in hushed tones that the person in question was actually very rich or they had won the lottery and suffered a breakdown, leading to their current circumstances. These things are seldom true, but one interesting case from Sunderland proves that is not always the case.

Lady Peat was a woman who lived for many years in a house in Villiers Street, and although she possessed considerable wealth, she was said to live in the cellar kitchen in a wretched state, sleeping inside a wooden box. The many other rooms in the property were elaborately furnished but were not seen to be occupied nor the windows ever clean.

As a youth she had married in pursuit of her desire to have a title and Sir Robert Peat, it is said, married her for her money, making it an arrangement that both found pleasing. Lady Peat received her title and Sir Robert Peat received £1,000 a year. Following the wedding ceremony, he returned down London, while she continued to live in Sunderland.

As if this story was not strange enough, it seems she was also a kleptomaniac and was widely known to be so. The local shopkeepers would pay her no heed, simply making a note of what the eccentric lady had stolen and sending the bill, which strangely was always paid. It is noted on one occasion she travelled to Herrington to collect a large sum of money owed by a tenant for rent, and when she was told to return the following week Lady Peat took some of the clothes from the washing line and put them in her bag. Two men who had witnessed the event took her back to the house and made her write off the money owed as well as pay for the clothes she had stolen.

Another bizarre tale from the life of Lady Peat states that at one time she invited a minister and a doctor round for tea with her. On sitting at her table, the servant announced they were out of tea, to which Lady Peat replied: 'There is some cold dumpling; just slice it and they will enjoy it, I know.' To which it is said the men did enjoy it.

When her husband eventually died it is reported that Lady Peat ran through the streets proclaiming the glorious news. Lady Peat herself passed away on 20 November 1842 and is now largely forgotten by the people of the town she once loved to steal from.

THE PRESIDENT'S DESK

The resolute desk has been used by the presidents of the United States of America since President Rushford B. Hayes in 1880. It was originally a gift from Queen Victoria 'as a memorial of the courtesy and loving kindness which dictated the offer of the gift'.

It is fashioned from the timber of HMS *Resolute*, a ship sent to find the John Franklin expedition and then abandoned in Melville Sound in 1854. The ship would later be found floating in Davis Strait, another

THE PRESIDENTS DESK

arm of the Arctic Ocean, by *George Henry*, an American whaling ship. After being returned back to England, the *Resolute* was repaired and served the Royal Navy for many more years.

When it was finally decommissioned, the oak timbers were repurposed to create a desk weighing more than 1,000lb. Since being given as a gift it has served in the first and second floor of the White House and most notably the Oval Office.

What is known by few, though, is that *Resolute* had been launched as a barque named *Ptarmigan*, which was built by Smiths of Shields on the Tyne in 1850.

WEEPING MADONNA

In October 1955 word spread of a miracle taking place in Walker, Newcastle. Mr and Mrs Taylor were said to be in possession of a plaster statue of the Virgin Mary and Jesus that had begun to weep.

Stories of weeping statues have long since drawn crowds wherever they have occurred in the world. All manner of liquids from oil to blood have been seen to drip from the faces of religious icons, leading many to claim a divine miracle has occurred.

Hundreds of faithful and curious people began descending on the Taylor residence in the hope of catching a glimpse of Newcastle's own miracle taking place. Mrs Taylor first noticed the phenomenon when glancing up at the figurine as it hung above her fireplace and noticing a tear slowly roll down its face. With people turning up to pray before the strange sight, one viewer even claimed the Madonna opened her eyes and wept.

Although the plaster figure had a humble beginning at the Newcastle Quayside, where it was purchased for 10s by Mrs Taylor, it would end up being a star attraction. It had hung in her previous home for ten years until disaster struck and a fire gutted the house. In an interesting turn of events the model was one of the only items saved from the incident, adding further lore to the now weeping statue.

The fame and attention eventually became too much for the humble Taylors and the throngs of crowds that were showing up every day, which were now being harassed by local youths. They were ordered to stop using their home as an exhibition space by the council. The story and the weeping statue have since faded into history, with the statue's location no longer known!

CANNIBALISM

The *Euxine* left the port of South Shields on 12 June 1884 carrying a cargo of coal. The ship ran into a fierce storm on 1 August that went on for days, resulting in one crew member falling overboard and drowning as the others watched helplessly. After a few days, the cargo ignited and while the ship's crew attempted to put the fire out they eventually had to abandon the ship in three lifeboats.

The captain managed to safely guide himself and another boat to the island of St Helena in the South Atlantic Ocean, but the third boat became separated. The remaining lifeboat contained seven members of the crew who had managed to rescue a small amount of provisions and water to last them until they found safety. After twelve days at sea, having lost sight of their friends, they decided to change course for Brazil in the hope of being spotted by another vessel.

Another few days passed as the sailors drifted at sea, and on 27 August some large waves capsized the boat multiple times. All navigation materials and rations were lost and things were beginning to look grim for the men. On 31 August a lottery was held, whereupon the 'winner' was to be killed and eaten so that some of the crew might stand a chance. It is reported a 20-year-old Italian man who only knew the English for yes and no had his number come up twice. When they went to draw a third time the boy refused, so someone drew for him only for his name to come up a third time. He submitted and allowed himself to be tied up and have his throat cut. It is said of the men that they drank the blood and ate his heart and liver before cutting off his hands and feet and throwing them overboard. The remainder of the body was stored to be eaten later.

Only a few hours later the crew were rescued by a passing ship. The events that took place on the boat were investigated, although no one was charged with any crime. The question of whether the lottery had actually ever taken place on board the small lifeboat among the lost and hungry men remains unanswered.

THE LEGEND OF THE MONK STONE

On the ancient road to Tynemouth Priory near Monk House Farm once stood a large stone pillar steeped in myth. The story of how the pillar came to be begins with a monk who was returning to the priory from an excursion. The monk, weary and hungry, came across the stately castle of the Delavals and entered.

Upon entering, the monk demanded food and refreshment, which was given to him by the servants of the castle. Lord Delaval was away hunting at the time and had ordered a pig to be roasted for him to

THE LEGEND OF THE MONK STONE

eat on his return. The greedy monk decided he would prefer to eat the pig, which, stunned by such a bold request, the servants refused. Deciding not to take no for an answer, the monk snatched a knife and decapitated the pig, quickly stuffing its head into a bag before fleeing the castle.

Lord Delaval returned from his hunting trip and was hastily informed of the shocking events. Infuriated by this, Delaval set off in pursuit of the thieving monk who was said to be a mile from the priory when he caught up. The monk was beaten so badly that he barely made it back to the priory, where he died shortly of his injuries.

Shocked by the death of the monk, the Church called for restitution and penance from Lord Delaval, who gave up some of his land to the priory. The stone originally marked the boundary between ecclesiastical land and civil land, although it was moved to the priory in 1936. The Monk Stone bears the inscription 'O horrid dede, to kill a man for a pigge's hede.'

Did you know Sunderland had its own strongman? Joseph Bessford, who gained the nickname Samson through his extraordinary feats of strength, was from the east end of Sunderland. Some of the things he was reported to have done were let a fire engine be driven over his chest, bend iron bars with his teeth and chew glass lightbulbs. He also competed in the British Strongman Championships but came second to a Mr Edwards.

CLARK, THE DEVIL

Born in 1787, Clark was a well-known character in the mid-Victorian period in North and South Shields. He kept a public house at the Cottage of Industry and Economy in Coble Dene and also owned a whiting manufactory. In one room of Clark's public house he exhibited coffins of his wife and children, who were still living at the

CLARK, THE DEVIL

time, with a coin slot and the option to donate should the funeral expenses become due.

In return for your donation you would receive a paper detailing some facts about Clark and his family. One of the facts recorded on the paper was that Clark's second wife had been buried in a chest that had been used as a case for a cuckoo clock.

He then married for a third time, and in case he should die he had 'grave clothes' made, which consisted of scarlet suits. It was said he loved to try on the suits and paraded the streets in the dark dressed as a devil. He was also reported to regret not having a pocket to hold his watch made into the suit, as he had no concern with time when he was meant to be wearing it.

Many members of Clark's family preceded him to the grave, unfortunately making his novel insurance policy rather useful. He later fell on hard times and left Coble Dene, moving to Milburn Place. It was here his third wife died and several of his children, leaving Clark, who was infirm, no other option than to enter the North Shields workhouse, where he died on 17 April 1870. Clark composed a toast to be drunk at his funeral, which went: 'Good meat and good drink, all for nothing, wishing poor Jack happy in heaven.' With which we will agree.

It would be interesting to see if one of Clark's papers survives today and could be given to a local museum. The last record of one surviving is 1946; perhaps it may still be out there, or even a different one is intact and stored in an unsuspecting person's home?

ANOTHER WIZARD OF THE NORTH

John Henry Anderson was born in July 1814 in The Mearns, near Aberdeen. Orphaned at the young age of 10, John joined a travelling dramatic company in 1830 and began his career, performing magic at the age of 17. He started his own touring show aged 23, which lasted three years, and then settled in London briefly, where it is believed Sir Walter Scott gave him the name the Great Wizard of the North.

Unlike Michael Scott mentioned in my last book and also referred to as the Wizard of the North, John is often credited with helping bring magic from a street art into theatres to entertain audiences. The bullet catch was perhaps his most well-known trick and though John did not invent it himself, it is believed a number of his rivals copied his technique. Another of his favourite tricks was to pull a rabbit from a hat, making him one of the first early magicians to popularise this trick. Touring Europe, Canada, America and many other places, he became well known for his intriguing craft. Later in his career he worked to expose fraudulent spiritualists by recreating their abilities, and he was one of the first people to expose the Davenport Brothers.

Anderson visited the North East a number of times during his long career, both as a stage performer and as part of his efforts to expose spiritualists. In one interaction in 1868 he sued a Newcastle man named John Richey, whom he had employed to post bills around town relating to his performances. When the Wizard of the North appeared in court to sue Richey for destroying the bills rather than posting them, he drew a great crowd of spectators. On another earlier visit in 1854 he writes fondly of the time he spent in Newcastle, addressing its residents in a letter sent to the *Newcastle Journal*. This quote is from that letter:

> In my various visits to this 'canny' town, ranging as they have done over a period of 27 years – from my first appearance as an unknown youth at the then Music Hall, in Blackett Street, to the time when last I had the honour of receiving the applause of a Newcastle audience – neither the number of my patrons, nor the approbation bestowed, nor the compliments received, have at any time equalled those with which it has been my good fortune to obtain at this my valedictory appearance.

The letter goes on to heap praise on Newcastle and its people as a city, leaving a distinct impression that despite his later quarrel over bill posting, Anderson still had great love for the city and the North East as a whole. Two of John's sons went on to become magicians and conjurers, one of whom, John Henry Anderson Jr, would have a dispute with his father over his career choice and they never spoke again. The Wizard of the North died at the Fleece Hotel in Darlington, County Durham, in 1874 and is buried in Aberdeen. Fellow magician Harry Houdini, who was born in the same year as Anderson's death, described him as one of his greatest inspirations and in 1909 arranged for the upkeep of his grave, which had fallen into disrepair.

AUTOMATONS

Self-operating machinery, such as the self-service checkout in most supermarkets, is something that in today's society is increasingly being taken for granted. However, it was only a short time ago when the marvel of a machine that could operate itself seemingly independently would have drawn crowds of eager spectators.

One interesting story of an automaton that is currently found in the North East is that of the Silver Swan. Created in approximately 1773 by John Joseph Merlin and a man named James Cox, its value was recognised immediately and it passed through a number of hands. While on display in Paris in 1867, American novelist Mark Twain came across it and wrote about it in his book *The Innocents Abroad*:

> I watched the Silver Swan, which had a living grace about his movement and a living intelligence in his eyes – watched him swimming about as comfortably and unconcernedly as if he had been born in a morass instead of a jeweller's shop – watched him seize a silver fish from under the water and hold up his head and go through the customary and elaborate motions of swallowing it …

The machine is believed to have been grander than its current form with a number of features having gone missing over the years. John Bowes purchased the swan in 1872 for £200 and it is currently in the Bowes Museum, County Durham, alongside a number of other automata collected by Josephine Bowes.

Did you know that the ancestors of George Washington, the first President of the United States, came from Washington in Tyne and Wear? Washington Old Hall, their family home, is a National Trust site and is open to the public.

FAMILY KEEPSAKE

The story you are about to read may be considered by modern eyes and ears to perhaps be a bit grotesque or horrid when it comes to a piece of family history, but nonetheless it is a tradition your parents or grandparents may be familiar with.

It is said that if during birth the child was born with some of the amniotic sack still covering its face, then this otherwise now useless waste product of the human body should in fact be kept. Folklore would have you believe that should a child be born with caul or veil, as it is more commonly known, then he or she are said to be lucky. Not only that but there is the belief among some that should a sailor take this to sea with them then they will not drown or die at sea.

My attention was first drawn to this strange bit of lore upon seeing a Facebook post in a North East group where a woman had shared a photograph of the veil that was covering her mother's face and had been kept in a box safe for over 112 years. To my surprise many others who commented had similar stories of relatives born with a veil. Something to think about should you have children on the way; it could well be a good omen at birth!

GOD ON THE TYNE

A bronze statue of the River God Tyne can be seen mounted on the wall of Newcastle Civic Centre, where it has been since its design by David Wynne for the centre's opening in 1968. The statue depicts the god, his face mostly hidden by hair and beard, with his arm outstretched.

GOD ON THE TYNE

A fountain of running water used to pour from the god's hand, but has not been in working condition for years.

But where does the idea of the River God Tyne come from? The idea of his sculpture originates from the designs for Somerset House, London, in 1786. The architect Sir William Chambers designed nine carved stone masks to hang on the building, to represent the ocean and eight of England's rivers. A wooden version was also carved in the early nineteenth century by Robert Sadler Scott and hung on a shop front in Grey Street, Newcastle.

The River God Tyne is usually depicted as having three plaits in his beard and wearing a basket on his head, filled with fish, coals, and workmen's tools, to represent the trade of Newcastle. The figure is said to refer back to the Roman belief that great rivers were home to deities who protected the communities around them. It is also a symbol of how integral the river was to the growing strength and trade of the city, as the River God Tyne is said to continue his watch over Newcastle's people to this day.

STRANGE EVENTS IN NILE STREET

In the summer of 1949, Mrs Harriet Clark of 51 Nile Street, Sunderland, was plagued by bizarre events taking place at her home. Harriet explained that she had witnessed two men in sand shoes climbing into her house during the early hours of the morning. If that isn't menacing enough, she found a note composed of newspaper headlines that had been stuck to an upstairs window that read: 'I Will Get Youse all.'

'It all began about a month ago,' she said. 'At about 1:30 a.m., we heard the back door creaking. One of the family ran out and found the back room light on, and the key from the door lying on the floor. There was no one there.' Since then the home had windows broken five times and their daughter had become too scared to stay the night. Mrs Clark became even more terrified after catching a glimpse of the face of a man through the window behind her bed head. Marks left on her kitchen window, which appeared to have been made by cigarettes, had also been found.

As this menacing campaign of harassment progressed, Harriet Clark found a parcel in the outhouse near the property. When the parcel was opened a blood-soaked shroud was found inside that appeared to be of expensive quality. Harriet put the parcel back where she found it and it vanished before the police arrived. Harriet's son-in-law, William MacDonald, then began house sitting in the hope of catching the perpetrators. After one of the incidents, William ran out the house and witnessed a man in sand shoes climbing out of the window of an empty house next door. He chased the man and his accomplice down, eventually catching him, but the man, who was described as being well spoken, explained they had been taking lead from the roof. William was knocked down and the two men escaped into the darkness.

The family continued to be tormented and the culprit's ability to avoid the police led some to believe they knew when they would be there. These strange goings on soon captured the public's imagination and it was reported to have drawn hundreds of people to the property, all desperate to have a look at the unexplainable. Harriet's daughter, Eva Clark, received a letter after the publication of the original article in the *Sunderland Echo* that read: 'People are wondering about the mystery of No. 51. But there is no mystery about it. We have been watching you for some time and we are out to get you.'

Eventually the family vacated the house to stay with relatives. No more seems to have been reported on these events, leaving them unexplained. Was it malicious thieves? Was it something paranormal? Or was it something else entirely?

FART LAMPS

When you picture street lamps being lit in days gone by, do you imagine a man with a tiny candle on a stick holding it aloft like a scene from a Dickens novel? Or can you picture nothing beyond the lamps that come on today, which mothers use to tell their bairns, 'Come home when the street lights come on.'

Well, there are in fact the remnants of another fuel-lit lamp still present in Whitley Bay today. Originally called gas destructor lamps, they were installed over 100 years ago; approximately ten of these still survive and can be seen dotted about on the streets.

As industry grew and spread, the build-up of deadly gases in the underground and sewers did too and they were becoming an increasing problem. Not only were these often poisonous, they were often highly flammable, too.

These gas destructor lamps were an innovative and ingenious solution to this problem, burning away the toxic sewer microbes and providing an efficient source of lighting to the public. There was, however, one issue, and this was that if the flame went out the lamps continued pumping the disgusting smell out into the atmosphere. Could our energy crisis see us return to pong power in the future? Or would this kick up too much of a stink?

SAWNEY BEAN

If you have seen a horror movie whose narrative concerns a group of inbred cannibals, chances are it has taken inspiration from the legend of Sawney Bean. While the truth of this tale is very much up for debate, its legacy lives on in popular culture today in fiction as stories of inbreeding and cannibalism seem eternally intertwined.

Alexander Sawney Bean is said to have been the head of a forty-five-person-strong clan that resided in Scotland and is thought to have been responsible for the murder and cannibalisation of a large number of unfortunate people. In a time before telephones, the internet and photographs, when keeping track of people was a much harder task, it was much easier for a person to simply disappear with little suspicion.

If you were a traveller during this period of time, making your way from Newcastle further north and into Scotland, there may well have been the chance that you would cross paths with this bloodthirsty group. The story of Sawney Bean really begins when he was a young man who, unwilling to follow in his father's footsteps as a ditch digger and hedge trimmer, left home with a woman of ill repute. The pair shared a nasty streak that would see them become social outcasts and, as if to further society's notion of them, they reportedly settled in a cave in Bennane Head on Scotland's coast.

The pair began to grow their clan, with Sawney and Agnes having eight sons, six daughters, eighteen grandsons and fourteen granddaughters over their twenty-five years living on the fringes of society. Numerous grandchildren were products of incest between their children. Not wanting to live an honest life, the group turned to crime, ambushing, robbing and murdering those who crossed their path.

The corpses of their victims were used as food to sustain them and, not being a wasteful bunch, they pickled anything they couldn't eat at the time, which would have most likely meant arms, legs and a few internal organs. That which was not eaten was banished to the sea, where it would wash up later, leading nearby villagers to suspect that an animal of some sort was responsible for the disappearances in the area.

Late one night the clan ambushed a husband and wife, much to their horror. The husband, being skilled with a sword and fortunate enough to be carrying a pistol, managed to fight off the attackers, whereas his wife was killed. As the clan fled, one member was caught and brought back to the village and interrogated. Likely under the force of torture, the clan member told the furious crowd where their lair was and it was not long before a plan of attack was drawn up.

Here is where the tale differs for many … some say the King sent in soldiers to rid the land of the scourge of Sawney Bean, who blew up the entrance to the cave with gunpowder, sealing the family in a tomb of their own making, and others say the clan surrendered and were executed without trial due to the animalistic nature of their crimes.

Regardless of what you believe, Sawney Bean is a bogeyman that has made those travelling alone wary and on guard. Did Sawney Bean ever exist? The likelihood is we will never know, but should you be travelling on your own up the northern coast at night, be sure to keep one eye on the caves.

QUACKERY

The term 'quack' when used to refer to a doctor is synonymous with knowingly promoting a medical treatment or cure when there is no proven health benefit. Originating from the Dutch word *quacksalver*, unlicensed practitioners often travelled up and down the county taking advantage of the desperate rich and poor alike.

In June 1776 a gang of such imposters were spotted in Newcastle trying to defraud its residents. Often investing money in handbills to raise awareness of their presence, the group, consisting of five main members, mainly hailed from Scotland and moved from town to town. They were deemed such a threat that their descriptions were reported in the *Newcastle Courant* following the successful arrest of one of the members.

Articles in the *North & South Shields Gazette* and *Northumberland and Durham Advertiser* in October 1852 describe how the markets were crammed with rival quacks hawking their goods, much to the annoyance of the locals. The money to be made in such an area is evident in the description provided in the article: 'Two of those fellows come driving down in well-horsed and fitted up dogcarts, and having in their persons adorned in the smartest mosaic jewellery.'

With little medicinal regulation, Britain was a popular target for such activities, and despite an attempt in 1748 to create a professional monitored status for doctors it was not until 1858 that this was successful. Things did not immediately change, however, and quackery could often result in a patient's death.

In 1863, Robert Brodie and Richard Lowes were remanded in Sunderland under the strong evidence of quackery having taken place. Brodie, a sawyer, and Lowes, a joiner, had conned a pilot in Monkwearmouth named James Atkinson into believing they were highly credited doctors. Brodie introduced himself as a doctor with three diplomas and charged the man a shilling to create a lotion, which he subsequently spent a penny on, purchasing the ingredients at the local chemist. He then brought Lowes along claiming he was his son, despite him being described as looking much older than Brodie, telling

Atkinson he was a star physician. It seems it did not take long for the imposters to be rumbled, as the pair were found sitting in a pub in Monkwearmouth by Atkinson's wife only a couple of days later.

THE LOST EXPLORER

Lieutenant Colonel Percy Fawcett was a renowned British geographer, archaeologist and explorer who was born in Torquay, Devon, in 1867. Often likened to an English Indiana Jones, Fawcett had served in the military in different parts of the world such as Ceylon and North Africa before undertaking expeditions in South America as an explorer.

Fawcett's early visits to South America were under the commission of the Royal Geographical Society with the aim of mapping the jungle. Numerous successful expeditions brought home tales of the dangers of the Amazon and the strange animals hidden within it. His success also meant he had gained a great deal of experience in the field and had also built up a relationship with some of the locals there. It was during his expeditions there that he came to the belief that located somewhere in the green inferno was hidden the Lost City of Z. The beginning of the First World War saw him drafted in to fight and he volunteered at Flanders and earned his rank, as well as being awarded the Distinguished Service Order in June 1917.

Following the war, thoughts of the Lost City of Z had not left Percy's mind, and after securing funding he returned to South America in 1925 determined to search once more. For this expedition his son Jack and Jack's best friend, Raleigh Rimmell, would accompany him into the unknown. Fawcett and his team went out into the thick Amazon jungle, never to be seen again, but a number of theories surrounding their disappearance began to surface. Some believed a tribe of violent natives had murdered the group, while others believed they were consumed by sickness or simply bested by the harsh environment.

Not everyone considered the group of British explorers dead, however, and rescue missions were launched, one of which resulted in the death of a fellow explorer. Fawcett's wealth of experience meant some held out hope for a good while, including one of his other sons, Brian Fawcett. Rumours of Fawcett going native and living in the jungle and bones found in the jungle believed to have been from members of the expedition team were dismissed by Brian, who held out hope for his brother Jack for years.

Brian Fawcett visited the North East a number of times to discuss tribal cultures and his father's expeditions. In March 1953 he came to Newcastle to host a talk on the missing expedition team before the release of a book made up of findings gathered by Percy Fawcett. He returned in January 1954, this time visiting the Whitley Bay Tea Club to host a talk on the Mystery of Matto Grosso, which he illustrated with slides. The final recorded visit I have found is some years later in 1960, when he appeared at the Tyne Hotel in Hood Street in Newcastle. For this talk he addressed the Newcastle upon Tyne and District Vegetarian Society on South American vegetarian tribes.

Despite a great deal of effort, no concrete evidence of the fate of the expedition team has been found since their disappearance. The events mentioned in this tale were recently portrayed on the big screen, with Newcastle-born actor Charlie Hunnam playing the role of Percy Fawcett. For further reading on the interesting story of Percy Fawcett I recommend David Grann's book *The Lost City of Z*, also the name of the movie, which gives more detail on the theories surrounding the expedition as well as the evidence that has surfaced. Almost 100 years later, the mystery of what happened to the team of British explorers who were swallowed by the jungle remains unanswered, and perhaps always will.

PEOPLE AND PLACES

Growing up in the North East, I think it can be very easy to struggle to see anything more than what we have here. Our self-deprecating humour is something we embrace, grumbling about how naff it is while we wait for a bus in the rain. Personally, I struggled to find any idols to look up to here. I wasn't into sports so football was out the question, and the only other person in the public spotlight was Cheryl Cole on *The X-Factor*. (Not that there is anything wrong with you Cheryl if you are reading this, I just didn't want to be you!)

Only when I started doing a bit of digging did I realise how many creative and talented people have come from and crossed paths with our patch.

SIAMESE TWINS

Siamese twins, or as they are now commonly referred to, conjoined twins, was a name that was made popular by Chang and Eng Bunker. The country of Siam, or Thailand as it is now known, was the birthplace of the two conjoined twins, who rocketed to fame because of their condition. Born in 1811, the two brothers went to the United States in 1829, performing in what would have then been labelled as freak shows. The two brothers quickly realised their potential and ditched their manager, deciding to take control of their own careers and tour on their own.

The two brothers visited Newcastle in May 1969. Bearing in mind that this was a time before the internet, television or radio, something as extraordinary as Siamese twins was likely unbelievable to many of the working-class folk. Hence, they drew great crowds of people wanting to see the conjoined twins for themselves. In reports of their visit it is said they conversed with locals, who at this point in their fifty-eight-year career sparked many questions.

Back home, the brothers had separate wives and would ultimately father twenty-one children between them, staying in different houses and swapping after three days. Prior to the Civil War the two kept slaves and after the defeat of the Confederate army the two lost a considerable amount of wealth.

Chang was the first to pass away at the age of 62 in 1874, with his brother following shortly after. What must it be like to be aware of your impending death?

WHITE HORSE

On a cliff in South Shields rests a painted white horse that has survived since the 1800s. Enduring the graffiti of youths down many generations, locals have repainted it regularly, but where did it start?

This is a rather interesting piece of local folklore. The first story I heard relating to the white horse was that a local soldier who fought in the Napoleonic Wars and lived nearby painted it to remind him of the horse he rode into battle.

This is far from the only story, though. One tale tells how a hunter got separated from his companions, being found dead alongside his white horse, and the painting commemorated the event.

Some tales date the horse even further back, with one story describing how Nestre, the daughter of a Saxon nobleman, fell for a Dane, whom she used to meet on Marsden beach. Rolf, her love, owned a white horse and one day it wandered off during their romantic encounter. This alerted Nestre's father, who was staunchly against their romance. An angry mob murdered the two lovers in a fury of passion and disapproval, with the mare being found later at the bottom of a cliff. It is thought the white horse was painted in commemoration out of regret and compassion.

Another tells how a stable boy, determined to impress his master, decided he would break a white mare against his advice. This effort failed miserably, and in a last-ditch effort for freedom the white horse raced off the cliff. The white horse in this tale was painted in memory of the master's favourite horse.

Each story will tell you something different, and if you read between the lines you can get an alternative meaning from each tale. It makes you ask who started each story and why?

THE OMEGA MAN

Star of such renowned films as the original *Planet of the Apes*, *The Omega Man* and *Soylent Green*, Charlton Heston is an actor renowned in his time. Although you may have seen some of his films, did you know that he can actually trace his roots back here to the North East?

Born John Charles Carter in the state of Illinois, Heston achieved Hollywood fame when he played the iconic role of Moses in *The Ten Commandments*. While there are many interesting facts relating to the life of this star of the big screen, I'll keep this relevant to us folks in the North East.

Heston's family originally arrived in North America in the 1600s, but his maternal great-grandparents, and namesake, are from the UK. His great-grandfather was William Charlton from Sunderland and his great -grandmother was Scottish. He emigrated to Canada, where his grandmother was born in 1872. In another twist of fate that would connect him to the North East, his grandfather was a miner who worked down the pits of Tyneside and Newcastle as a boy before emigrating to the US.

Heston would return to the North East a number of times over the years, to star in plays like *The Greatest Show on Earth*, research his family history in Jesmond and attend the reopening of the Theatre Royal in Grey Street, Newcastle, in 1988.

During a press conference at the reopening, Heston said:

My grandfather came from the Newcastle area. He worked in the mines as a boy of eight or nine around 1890 to 1895. He emigrated to America soon after with his mother.

I believe Carter is not an uncommon name in Newcastle, although I don't know of any relatives who might still be living here.

So there you have it. Charlton Heston, named after a Mackem relative with a grandad who worked down the pits in Newcastle.

VESTA TILLEY

For those of you inclined to visit the Empire Theatre in Sunderland, Vesta Tilley may well be a name that rings a bell. On the side of the building sits a stone that reads: 'This stone was placed by Miss Vesta Tilley. Sept 29th 1906.'

But who is Miss Vesta Tilley?

Tilley, real name Matilda Alice Powles, was an English stage actress and performer who began her career in 1869. With her father as her manager, she played theatres all over the country and even overseas in the United States on the Vaudeville circuit. She would become best known for being a male impersonator in drag including principal boy in pantomime acts, which is when an actress would play the young male protagonist.

By the 1890s Tilley had become one of, if not the, highest-paid women in the entire country. In 1906 she would visit Sunderland to lay the foundation stone at the Empire Theatre, recognised as theatre royalty and being presented a silver jewelled casket and jewelled tray. In a cavity under the foundation stone was deposited copies of the *Sunderland Echo* and *The Era*, a newspaper devoted to the entertainment industry, as well as a number of coins of the realm.

Upon the placing of the stone, Tilley is quoted as saying: 'I declare this stone to be well and truly laid, and I wish every success may attend the building of which it is part.'

The theatre itself would open less than a year later, in 1907. Tilley would go on performing until 1920 and was recognised during the First World War as being a recruiting tool due to her patriotic songs.

HADRIAN AND HIS WALL

The most famous wall in the North East, stretching all the way from Wallsend to Bowness-on-Solway in the west, first came into being in AD 142 when construction began during the Roman occupation of Britain under the rule of the then Emperor Hadrian.

It is thought to have been built for a number of reasons, such as to establish a series of customs posts, to determine Britannica's borders and most of all as a defensive measure.

When the Romans arrived in Britain the country was home to a number of warring tribes that all commanded their own patch of the country and were struggling for power. The Roman military allied with a number of these tribes but could not conquer the far north!

Emperor Hadrian was well travelled and would venture across the Roman Empire for over a decade of his twenty-five-year reign implementing plans to improve and strengthen it, rather than having the sole goal to expand it further.

Considered a show of power and arguably the strongest part of his legacy, parts of the wall are still standing today and can be visited by the public. Even in recent times, during construction work on Newcastle city centre, parts of the wall have been uncovered buried below the concrete surface.

Hadrian would die at the age of 62, with some concluding a heart attack was responsible. In his later years he would compose poetry and this is one of his works:

Animula, vagula, blandula
Hospes comesque corporis
Quae nunc abibis in loca
Pallidula, rigida, nudula,
Nec, ut soles, dabis iocos.

Little soul, you charming little wanderer, my body's guest and partner,
Where are you off to now?
Somewhere without colour, savage and bare;
Never again to share a joke.

DANIEL DEFOE

Along the footpath from Hillgate up to the Sage in Gateshead you are likely to spot a plaque dedicated to Daniel Defoe (1660–1731).

He is considered by some to be the father of the British novel, with perhaps his most notable work being *Robinson Crusoe* in which a castaway finds himself on a beach in South America encountering cannibals, captives and mutineers.

Defoe lived in Gateshead between 1706 and 1710, with his lodgings believed to have been in Hillgate. Some say he was hiding away in the North East from debt collectors, and it is also alleged he wrote some of *Robinson Crusoe* while up here. It begs the question if any Geordies from down the quayside inspired his tall tale?

INVENTOR OF THE LIGHT SWITCH

John Henry Holmes was an electrical engineer, Quaker and inventor who was born in 1857. Spending some of his youth studying at Friends School in Bootham in York, at the age of 16 he attended an entrance exhibition at what was then Durham College of Science. Two short years later he became an apprentice at Head, Wrightson and Co. of Stockton-on-Tees, where he began handling electrical equipment. Although John would have previously had some education in the field, he would became famous as an electrical engineer despite not attending any specific course in the field.

In 1880 he attended a public demonstration of Joseph Swan's incandescent light bulb, which is believed to have sparked his interest in electrical lighting. Despite contacting Swan a number of times in the hopes of becoming his apprentice, it never happened. In 1883, John and his brother Theodore founded J.H. Holmes & Co. in the Shieldfield area of Newcastle. The company specialised in early motors, dynamos, switches and lighting. In 1884 the first Holmes dynamo was built and it was also this same year that Holmes invented the quick-break light switch. The mechanism, still used in light switches today, was revolutionary as it increased the life of switches by reducing the time lag of the contacts coming together, and it was also considered less of a fire hazard. The company also installed Newcastle's first domestic electrical lighting at their father's house, who also lived most of his life in Tyne and Wear.

In 1889, Holmes travelled to Egypt to study the requirements of vessels passing through the Suez Canal by night. Following his research, he designed and supplied portable lighting apparatus that increased the canal's use during dark hours. He also went on to supply installations in Europe and the British colonies, making deals in America as well.

Holmes passed away in 1935 and while he is little remembered in our time, the contributions he made to the world are still evident today. At the Discovery Museum in Newcastle a reconstruction of Holmes's workshop is on display featuring some of his original tools and early lamps with more information. Light switches are just one of the many pieces of technology we take for granted today, but to those from Tyne and Wear it is one more reason to take pride in our area.

THE MARRIAGE OF LORD BYRON

George Gordon Byron, known as Lord Byron, was born in 1788 in London and was the son of a British Army officer and writer. Known largely for being a leading figure in the Romantic movement, Byron's life was considered scandalous at the time and he became a person of notoriety. His reputation for having affairs with both men and women prior to his marriage saw him travel in Europe, the Mediterranean in particular, to avoid former lovers and in the hope of gaining new experiences.

Byron's work had put him in the spotlight as someone who great things were expected of and many of his poems, such as 'Childe Harold's Pilgrimage', published in 1812, saw his popularity increase. Pressed by debt and numerous scandals from former lovers, he sought a suitable marriage to calm the rising tensions. As 1815 was just beginning Byron arrived in Seaham for his wedding to Annabella Millbank, which would take place at Seaham Hall. Two years prior to this, rumours had begun to circulate about an incestuous relationship between Byron and his half-sister, Augusta Leigh, with whom he had only just reconnected after not seeing her for four years. His wife to be, Annabella, was said to be the likely inheritor to her rich uncle's fortune and the marriage would arguably be of great benefit to Byron.

Following Byron's marriage, he fathered a daughter named Ada, who was born in December that year. However, their marriage was short-lived due to the numerous affairs and scandals linked to him, and by 1816 Annabella had left him, taking her daughter with her. The publicity of the separation combined with rumours of his incestuous relationship with his sibling and the burden of his debt saw him leave Britain in April 1816, never to return.

His travels saw him befriend Percy Shelley and his future wife, Mary Godwin. While trapped inside together due to bad weather in Ville Diodati in Switzerland, Mary would conceive her idea for the now well-known novel *Frankenstein*. Byron continued his travels across Europe, with many of the places he visited erecting monuments to the time he spent there in recent years. His gradual release of *Don Juan*, perhaps his most famous work, resulted in criticism for its immorality but did not stop its popularity. Byron went on to board the *Hercules* in Genoa, which had set off only a few miles from Seaham Hall, and travelled to Greece, where his support for its fight against the Ottoman Empire would make him a national hero to this day.

While in Greece, Byron developed a violent fever and passed away in 1824. Although his life was considered immoral by many and he was constantly judged, he is remembered fondly for the impact he had on each place he visited and for the great works he produced as a romantic poet.

THE CAT AND DOG STEPS

On the coast of Seaburn leading down to the sea is a set of stone steps that have long been called the cat and dog steps. While I cannot find any conclusive proof as to why they are there, there are some grim stories told by locals as an explanation for the name.

In the past, before vets were a common sight on the high street and some of the residents of Sunderland with less money had pets, it was not usual to have them neutered. As such, families could often be burdened with a litter of kittens or puppies that they simply could not afford to take care of. While we have different views of animals now, what would be seen as mercy then was taking them to those steps and holding them under the water by the sea so as to prevent a life of suffering. Another explanation for the name is that the killing was carried out further up the River Wear and the remains would be washed down to these particular steps.

DOG LEAP STAIRS

The Dog Leap Stairs are a staircase in the centre of Newcastle that have been immortalised in folklore by the role they played in a controversial love story. John Scott was the son of a local merchant who was born in Newcastle in 1751. John had fallen in love with Bessie Surtees, the daughter of a banker, whose father disapproved. Bessie's father arranged for her to be married to another suitor, prompting them into desperate action.

On a cold night in November 1772, John and an old friend arrived on horseback outside Bessie's house in the dead of night with a ladder. She climbed out of her first-floor bedroom window and onto John's horse before the two escaped up the narrow staircase. The pair fled to Scotland, where they married against the wishes of both families and then returned to England. Before long, Bessie's father accepted what he could not change and both families reconciled.

John later went on to become Lord Chancellor of England and was ennobled to become Lord Eldon. Eldon Square stands in his memory, although his reputation was tarnished after he was held responsible for a tragic conflict with protesters in Manchester in 1819 that became known as the Peterloo Massacre. The protesters, who were urging social reform and an end to corruption, were set upon by cavalry. At least eleven people died and hundreds were injured, with the public holding Lord Eldon as one of the people responsible for the atrocity. Lord Eldon played an important role in the repressive government of the time by using his power to push through legislation that allowed imprisonment of the enemies of the Tory party.

The stairs were relocated in the 1890s when the area went through construction changes for the railway.

HARLEM COFFEE COOLER

Frank Craig, also known as the Harlem Coffee Cooler, was a late nineteenth-century African American boxer born in 1868. Craig began fighting professionally in the 1890s and was declared coloured middleweight champion of America in 1894 after defeating Joe Butler. However, he did not defend his title and travelled to England instead. Craig followed in the footsteps of Peter Jackson, also known as the Black Prince, who crossed the Atlantic from Australia and achieved celebrity status and success in Europe.

Frank Craig stayed in England for five years, boxing up and down the country as much as he could and even fighting eleven times in one month at one point. After becoming middleweight champion of England, Craig briefly returned to America, where a series of losses swiftly brought him back to Britain. Once here he eventually made his way to the North East.

In August 1900, Craig appeared in a local music hall in Sunderland. Craig made his regular offer of £5 to anyone who could last three rounds with him. A shipyard worker, who was considered to be a local favourite, accepted the offer and stepped into the ring. The Harlem Coffee Cooler knocked the man out in seconds, causing an uproar as the audience saw their champion on his back. It is reported an orange was hurled with such velocity that when it hit Craig it briefly knocked him unconscious. The victor quickly stumbled to his feet and fled to the dressing room while the angry crowd mobbed the stage. The safety curtain was dropped to disperse the mass of furious shipyard workers but the rioting continued for several hours and resulted in an acrobat, who resembled Craig and had been travelling with him, being assaulted.

The Harlem Coffee Cooler continued to fight until 1912, with many of his bouts occurring in Newcastle and surrounding areas. Ten years after his retirement he staged a one-night-only, three-round comeback fight against Jim Rideout, which he lost on a decision. The legendary boxer died in Chelsea in 1943 and held a final record of 68-36-9.

LISTEN EAR

The War of Jenkin's Ear is perhaps one of the more obscure chapters in the UK's military history and as such it is largely forgotten. At a time when the country's relationship with Spain was frosty to say the least, with British ships in the Americas being boarded and searched for slaves in a bid to control the trade, it was not uncommon for tales such as the one we are about to hear to leak out from that part of the world.

Robert Jenkins was a British ship's captain whose vessel was boarded by the Spanish in search of contraband in 1731. In the hope of preventing slaves being transported and sold outside their control, they ransacked the ship and, according to Jenkins, cut off his ear, leaving it with him aboard his vessel, the *Rebecca*.

Some years passed and England's relationship with Spain deteriorated as England also established colonies such as Georgia, which led to the resurfacing of the story of Jenkins and his mistreatment by the Spanish. The irony of this being in relation to slave trading in the Americas is not lost on me, and how it is possible to make such an issue of one man losing his ear while many were suffering in chains is beyond me, but this was the eighteenth century. Jenkins was summoned to Parliament in London and paraded before a crowd with his shrivelled ear in a jar, telling the story of how his ship was boarded and his ear removed.

When asked in the House of Commons, 'What did you do?' Jenkins replied, 'I commended my soul to God and my cause to my country.'

Although it had taken place some years earlier, the assault on Jenkins was seen as an assault on the country and war began against Spain with a naval attack. Without boring you with every detail of the resulting nine-year conflict, let me say that there were many casualties, particularly for the British, with the total estimated at 30,000. The war itself would become subsumed by the Austrian War of Succession in 1748.

One man from Newcastle did try and barter for peace, however, and his name was Thomas Pelham Holmes, the 1st Duke of Newcastle. Public opinion would see this made impossible, largely in part due to the support for the war across the country. In a U-turn, perhaps to prove himself a patriot, the duke then threw himself into supporting the war, with one of his notable suggestions being the use of previously untapped resources from the American colonies. If you can't beat 'em, join 'em, ey?

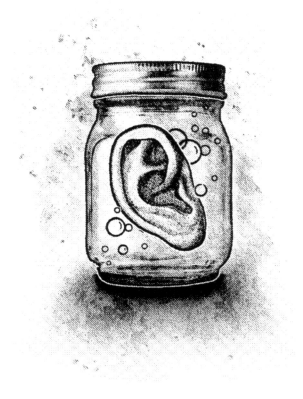

LISTEN EAR

A NIGHT AT THE OPERA

In Croft Avenue, Sunderland, sits a relatively new blue plaque celebrating the childhood home of Ida and Louise Cook, who were two sisters born only a few years apart in the early 1900s. The sisters, who had a passion for opera, are recognised for their efforts in helping people of the Jewish faith escape the tyranny of the Nazi regime.

Under the pseudonym of Mary Burchell, Ida became a prolific writer who used her funds to visit Austrian and Germanic opera with her sister, saving not only the possessions of those facing the wrath of the dictatorship but the lives of those simply looking for the right to exist. Travelling out in simple clothing, the two would return in the jewellery and furs of those they were trying to help.

Many years later, Ida said: 'The funny thing is we weren't the James Bond type – we were just respectable Civil Service typists.'

The things one considers as basic human duty at the time may later be recognised as a heroic effort. Are we good because someone is watching or because it is the right thing to do? Ask yourself that.

THE CARNEGIE CONNECTION

Andrew Carnegie was a Scottish-American industrialist who led the expansion of the American steel industry in the late nineteenth century, and is often identified as one of the richest people ever. He was also a famous philanthropist and during the last eighteen years of his life he gave away approximately 90 per cent of his wealth, funding education, music halls and over 3,000 libraries around the world.

In October 1908, Sunderland's first branch library opened in Hendon thanks to his generosity. This is one of three that would be built in Sunderland: Hendon, Monkwearmouth and West Branch (Kayll Road library). Carnegie even attended the Monkwearmouth library opening himself on 21 October 1909.

He once famously said: 'No man will make a great leader who wants to do it all himself, or to get all the credit for doing it.'

WILLIAM THOMAS STEAD

William Thomas Stead was born in Northumberland in 1849 and was a pioneer in the field of investigative journalism. He was best known for his 1885 series of articles, *The Maiden Tribute of Modern Babylon*, written in support of a bill to raise the age of consent from 13 to 16, dubbed the Stead Act. He also produced the children's book series *Books for Bairns*.

During the 1890s he took a particular interest in spiritualism and said he was in contact with the spirit world. It was said he was able to produce automatic writing, claimed to be a psychic ability.

He was aboard *Titanic* the fateful night it sank. Survivors reported little about his final hours, but it is said that after the ship struck an iceberg he helped women and children into lifeboats and gave away his lifejacket to another passenger. A later sighting saw him clinging to a raft, although his body was not recovered.

Stead frequently said he would die of either drowning or lynching. His earlier fictional publications relating to the sinking of two ships with high loss of life gained significant attention after his death in light of his spiritual connections.

Ten years after *Titanic* sank, his daughter published a book in which Stead describes his death and discusses the afterlife. The manuscript was produced using automatic writing, and Ms Stead cited as proof of its authenticity the writer's habit of going back to cross 't's and dot 'i's while proof reading, which she said was characteristic of her father's writing technique in life.

Did you know that the band Queen played in Sunderland? In March 1974 they visited the Locarno Ballroom at the Mecca in Roker. They played on the same day their album *Queen II* was released.

SISTER WINIFRED LAVER

Winifred Laver was born in Birkenhead in 1888 to a well-to-do family. She came to Gateshead at the age of 18 and in 1916 she established the Vine Street Mission after seeing people living in poverty in other parts of the country. At the time Gateshead had the worst record for tuberculosis in the country and her family did not want her to take the position. However, being a Methodist, she believed it is where God wanted her to be.

Sister Winifred worked tirelessly for over sixty years providing food, shelter and clothing to those less fortunate than herself, as well as working with children whose parents had been killed in war. During her time working at the mission she never received a salary and lived entirely off her family legacy.

Sister Winifred Laver died in 1980 aged 92. She was awarded an MBE for her amazing work and her legacy is commemorated by a blue plaque in Gateshead.

ARBEIA ROMAN FORT

Arbeia was a large Roman fort built in AD 160 at the mouth of the Tyne in South Shields. It was used as a maritime supply base for the many garrisons at Hadrian's Wall while the Romans were in Britain.

While there is evidence the ruins of the fort had been known about since the 1600s, the first excavation did not take place until 1875. Since then civilian settlements have been uncovered in areas near to the fort and it is now one of the most extensively excavated sites of its kind in the former Roman Empire.

The now partially reconstructed site houses a museum containing many of the fascinating finds that have been discovered over the years. In the nearby pub, the Lookout Inn, stories of ghostly Roman soldiers in full armour have also been reported, leading some to believe that the Romans are not done with South Shields yet.

THE GREAT FIRE OF NEWCASTLE AND GATESHEAD

During the early hours of 6 October 1854, a small fire began on the Gateshead side of the Tyne at the Worsted Manufactory. At the time gaslight was used to see and could have been a possible cause for the ignition. The building was said to contain wool and oil, and this helped the fire to spread quickly to the warehouse next door, which also contained flammable materials.

A crowd began to gather to watch the spectacle from the other side of the river, with some people on the river itself. The warehouse soon exploded when the fire spread, the chemicals shooting blue flames into the sky and scattering heavy debris for ¾ mile. A contemporary report said:

> Articles of every description were thrown up with the force of a volcanic eruption, only to fall with corresponding momentum upon the dense masses of the people assembled and upon the surrounding habitations.

The fire engulfed homes and businesses alike, and quickly began to spread across the Newcastle side of the river. The city quickly issued a plea for help and fire engines arrived from Sunderland, Hexham, Durham, Morpeth and Berwick. Fifty-three people were recorded as losing their lives in the tragedy, with many more seeing their homes destroyed.

THE VICTORIA TUNNELS

The Victoria Tunnels are a subterranean wagonway network that runs beneath the streets of Newcastle upon Tyne.

It was built in 1839–42 to transport Newcastle's biggest export at that time, coal, from the main colliery in Spital Tongues down to the river, where it would be loaded onto boats for export.

The tunnel is a whopping 2.4 miles long, at its deepest it is 85ft and it drops 222ft from entrance to exit.

Mining is a dangerous occupation though, and the tunnels were no different. This tale of the death of William Coulson, an inspector, illustrates this.

As I have said, the tunnels were a wagonway, with heavy loads passing up and down constantly. This particularly gruesome incident was the result of wagons being sent down the tunnel without those in charge being aware that three surveyors were inside the tunnel at the bottom end carrying out an inspection.

The party of surveyors, much to their horror, heard the noisy rattle of the wagons approaching them. The three inspectors had very little time to decide on a plan of action. Packed close together with little to no hope of escape, their options were severely limited. The three men made very different decisions when faced with life or death. One man chose to run, hoping to get out of their entrapment, one decided that he would hug the wall and hope the wagons would go past him, and the last man chose to lie down between the tracks, hoping that the carts would travel over him.

If you have ever visited Victoria Tunnels, which are open to tours, you can get a sense of the sheer terror these three men must have felt at the danger barrelling towards them.

Lady Fortuna spun her wheel and the three men sealed their own fate. It was the man who tried to run that was killed first as he could not clear the distance in time. The man who chose to press himself against the wall was severely injured, while the man who lay down on the tracks, perhaps the riskiest move of the three, escaped without injury.

The tunnels closed in 1860; however, during the Second World War they were used as an air raid shelter, with many families seeking refuge in them. They are now open and can be toured.

EARL GREY

Built in 1838, Grey's Monument is a Grade I listed commemoration of Earl Charles Grey in Newcastle city centre. The statue is 130ft high and features a sculpture of Lord Grey standing on top. The sculpture was

EARL GREY

designed by Edward Hodges Baily, the same creator of Horatio Nelson's monument in Trafalgar Square.

Earl Charles Grey was Prime Minister between 1830 and 1834. He is most famously recognised for his government overseeing the abolition of slavery in the British Empire.

In September 1941 the monument was struck by lightning and the head was blown off, landing on a passing tram below. The Earl stood decapitated for seven years before finally getting a new head. As well as his impact on slavery, Earl Grey is also well known for having a blend of tea named after him.

AN INFLUENCE ON CHARLES DARWIN

William Paley, clergyman, utilitarian and philosopher, was born in Peterborough in 1743. Destined for a life intertwined with academia due to his family connections, he soon found his place in the Church and moved around the country holding different positions in the hierarchy before eventually arriving in Sunderland, which at the time would have been Bishopwearmouth.

He would become rector of Bishopwearmouth, HQ St Michael and All Angels Church, now Sunderland Minster, between 1796 and his death in 1805. During these years he would pen a theological work, which is still in discussion today.

Paley's final work, *Natural Theology or Evidences of the Existence and Attributes of the Deity*, would propose the watchmaker analogy. In simple terms, this argued that should you see a rock on a beach you would not understand how it had been created, however if you were to look at a watch you would understand that due to its complex nature it has a creator. He argued this was the case with the human body and the eyes.

Whilst science has unraveled many mysteries of the world in the 200 years since this argument's conception, the notion of a divine creator being involved in the complexity of life is one that is still present in theological and philosophical debate.

Some of you may remember that old man we had on the £10 note? Yes, that's right – Charles Darwin! Famous for his theory of evolution, Darwin was well aware of William Paley's work Throughout his lifetime he disproved many of the Sunderland philosopher's propositions after Paley's death, arguing that there is nothing accidental when it comes to evolution.

Richard Dawkins, the renowned British evolutionary biologist, even tipped his hat to Paley in his 1986 book *The Blind Watchmaker*, which highlights the relevance of his work all these years later.

With Paley having spent a good part of time of his life in Sunderland, it is very likely a large part of this theory was penned here. With this being very possible, it begs the question was it a beach in Sunderland where he had seen a rock that helped propel this theory?

THE HERMIT OF COQUET ISLE

Said to be a Dane of noble birth, Henry Coquet's story begins with a marriage being forced on him by his parents in Denmark. Having other desires, Henry fled his homeland and came to Tynemouth, with the exact date of him arriving in the North East a mystery.

Guided by a vision from God, he gained permission from the priory to create a cell on an island off the Northumberland coast. Here, the noble Dane lived in isolation, cultivating crops, with locals murmuring that the hermit had the gift of second sight. Throughout history the 'other,' the 'stranger', is often described as being different in a way that separates us and them, which may well have been the case with Henry here.

With that said, there were stories that surrounded Henry the hermit, such as knowing when his half-brother was killed back in Denmark or foreseeing a ship being swallowed by the stormy sea. In one example of his strange talent, it is said he told a drunken monk the last date and time the man had indulged himself in a drink.

In John Crawford Hodgson's *A History of Northumberland*, issued under the direction of the Northumberland County History Committee (1899), one tale of him leaving his hermitage in aid of a fellow man of God can be read:

A priest in the immediate neighbourhood was lying dangerously ill: as St. Henry approached his house he heard the demons gloating over their sure possession of his soul, alleging the priest had only done one good deed in all his life. With some difficulty he convinced them that the one good deed was of such a nature as to outweigh all the bad ones; such was their disappointment that the demons placed no further hindrance in the way of the priest's recovery and reformation. Except for a pilgrimage to Durham, to the shrine of the saint he strove to emulate, this is the only mention of St. Henry quitting his island.

Henry Coquet died in 1127 and is venerated by the Catholic Church, being more commonly known as St Henry the Dane. In the church of St Thomas in Canterbury there is a stained-glass window depicting St Henry in his horned helmet.

THE DEAD HOUSE

In Ouseburn near the mouth of the Tyne once stood a building named the Dead House. The small building consisted of two rooms, one for dead bodies, the other for the resident attendant. Bodies that had been found in the Tyne would be brought here to be stored and identified if possible.

Cuckoo Jack, also known as John Wilson, was a local bargeman hired by the council to collect the numerous bodies that would be found floating in the river. Cuckoo Jack was paid by the body, and is thought to have been responsible for dredging and delivering over 200 to the Dead House.

Without the safety precautions that today seem obvious, accidents around the Tyne were frequent. There was no safety rail to protect the public and it was easy to stumble and fall into the river. Over time the rate at which bodies were discovered gradually decreased and in 1906 the Dead House was demolished.

> **Did you know**, as someone who plays video games I have always been keeping my eye out for some kind of *Grand Theft Auto Tyne and Wear*. Well, the PlayStation 1 game *Driver* may be the closest we will get. While the game actually covers four cities, which are Miami, San Francisco, Los Angeles and New York, Newcastle is included as a secret bonus that can be accessed via cheat codes.

SUFFRAGETTES IN NEWCASTLE

This year marks the 100th anniversary since women first got the right to vote; however, it was a long and difficult struggle before the movement progressed to that point. On 9 October 1909 a demonstration was planned in Newcastle opposing an event where Lloyd George, the Chancellor of the Exchequer, was due to speak. The event took place at the Palace Theatre near the Haymarket with tickets specifying that they were 'Not to be sold to a woman'.

The event saw a huge police presence drafted in, with the area surrounding it being roped off and undercover policemen in plain clothes from London mingling in with the crowd. However, this did not stop the demonstrators from making their voice heard.

Winifred Jones broke the window of one of the Palace Theatre doors. Lady Constance Lytton threw a stone at Sir Walter Runciman's car that had the following message attached: 'To Lloyd-George, Rebellion Against Tyranny is Obedience to God. Deeds, not Words.' Emily Wilding Davison also attempted to throw a projectile but was arrested by a plainclothes policeman as she got the stone from her pocket. Another incident occurred when Jane Brailsford hid an axe within a bouquet of flowers, intent on destroying the barriers holding the crowd back. Later that day, Dorothy Pethick and Kitty Marion entered the General Post Office and broke a number of windows, resulting in their arrest. The suffragette activist Emily Davison, who later died after stepping in front of the King's horse at the Epsom Derby, was also in attendance.

Davison was released without charge but those mentioned and other women were sentenced and held in Newcastle Gaol. Together they went on hunger strike, resulting in their force-feeding via a tube up the nostril. Lady Lytton was released as she was deemed unfit to remain in the prison. The last to be set free was Kitty Marion on 10 November after a month of imprisonment. During this time she was said to have barricaded her cell door and blocked the aperture of the door with a handkerchief to stop officials being able to view her. She also struck the doctor tasked with feeding her, telling him there was not an ounce of manliness in him. Following this she started a fire in her cell using a Bible as kindling, which resulted in her passing out and awaking in a padded cell.

After her release she was met at the gates by a number of local leaders of the suffragette movement and was reported as being in good spirits. This story only touches on a small amount of the hardships these activists went through in the strive for equality, as many other stories about their local efforts are out there. Although women did receive the right to vote in 1918, it only applied to women over 30 and men over 21. It was not until 1928 that women aged 21 and over would also be granted their right to vote, which is also another anniversary we look forward to celebrating.

EDDIE KIDD – STUNTMAN

Edward Kidd was born in Islington, London, in 1959 and from the young age of 14 began performing motorcycle stunts for captivated audiences. Eddie's amazing skills would see him double for actors such as Harrison Ford, Michael Caine and even Pierce Brosnan as James Bond in *GoldenEye*. Despite not having a licence for the approximate 12,000 jumps he had made in his career until 1995, Kidd managed to set a number of world records and perform amazing feats.

Considered by many to be Britain's greatest stunt performer, he was challenged by the late Evel Knievel's son, Robbie, to a motorcycle jump-off in 1993 as Robbie deemed him the only person worthy of the competition, which he won. Some of his other memorable stunts included jumping over the Great Wall of China and setting a world record for jumping over fourteen double-decker buses in 1978, beating Evel Knievel's record.

Kidd made a few appearances in the North East during his career, including a spot on *Byker Grove*, of which he was reportedly a fan. He stood in as a stunt double for PJ, played by Anthony McPartlin, somersaulting off a three-wheeled motorcycle in Chopwell Woods in 1992. Aside from this he also performed stunt shows as part of a tour, including one in Bents Park, South Shields, in 1981.

In August 1996, Kidd suffered a tragic accident while performing at Long Marston Airfield near Stratford-upon-Avon. Although he made the initial jump, his chin struck the petrol tank of the motorcycle, knocking him unconscious. This prevented him stopping the bike quickly. He continued up over an embankment and the resulting fall left him paralysed and with brain damage. His courage has not left him, however, as he completed the 2011 London Marathon and also carried the Olympic Torch in 2012.

TITANIC

Perhaps the most infamous ship to have ever been lost at sea, the story of *Titanic* is one that has fascinated the public for generations. Charles William, born in Sunderland 1881, spent his early years in what is now recognised as the Millfield area likely living in a crowded house with a large number of siblings and half-siblings. Picking a trade of which Sunderland had a booming industry for at the time, he became involved in glassworks and became a glass bender before moving to London aged 19.

Having worked his way up his employer's hierarchy, William no doubt believed he was going on a once-in-a-lifetime trip when he purchased the ticket for the doomed *Titanic* voyage, not knowing how true this would be. His second-class return ticket would see him board at Southampton to crowds of onlookers waving goodbye to friends and relatives, unaware of the fateful events to come.

William would later describe the clash with the icy behemoth that would ultimately sink the ship:

> A party of four of us had been smoking and playing cards in the second cabin smoking room when the shock came. There was a man named Fox, a Texas ranchman, one other man, and myself.
>
> We felt a slight jar and hastened to the deck. Even as we did so, we saw the iceberg, huge and white against the dark blue sea, go whizzing past on the starboard side of the ship, just clear of the stern.
>
> We returned immediately to the smoking room and finished our game of cards. By that time we could hear many voices on deck and again went out to learn what had happened.
>
> Officers were telling everyone that there was no danger and no reason to worry in the least.

This would prove deadly advice if adhered to and William ultimately fetched his lifejacket and managed to board lifeboat no. 9.

In harrowing detail, he described what came next:

> We rowed about 400 yards from the ship before we saw her settling slowly by the head. Then there was an explosion. The lights went out and the ship seemed to break, her nose plunging down and her stern bucking almost straight up.
>
> I put my hands over my ears to shut out the wailing as the lights went out, and those on board began to realise that something dreadful was going to happen. The screams grew fainter and fainter very soon, however.
>
> Later in the morning, when we were aboard the *Carpathia*, I saw many of the bodies floating by.

In the end it would be a ship built right here in the North East that would ultimately go on to save the lives of many of those fortunate enough to escape the terrifying ordeal.

The passenger steamship RMS *Carpathia* came to the rescue. It had been built in Wallsend at Swan Hunter & Wigham Richardson shipyard, begging the question of whether William may have had a friendly face from the North East to natter to on his journey to home and safety.

> **Did you know** the River Tyne used to be home to a number of islands? The largest of these was called Kings Meadow Island and it even had its own pub at one point named the Countess of Coventry. Horse and greyhound racing would take place on the island and during the siege of Newcastle in 1644 Scottish sentries were posted there, shooting dead at least one unfortunate sailor who tried to make it past them.
>
> The island, along with smaller islands such as one named Little Annie that lay nearby, were removed in the 1800s to make it easier for shipping traffic to pass through.

CARL HERMAN UNTHAN

Carl Herman Unthan was born in Sommerfield, East Prussia, in 1848 without arms. His father was employed as a teacher and encouraged Carl to be independent. Some stories state that he could feed himself by the age of 2 and began playing the violin at 10, showing potential almost immediately. When he turned 16 he attended a music conservatory. He graduated a couple of years later and began touring.

By the time Carl was in his 20s he was touring to packed theatres, eventually arriving in the North East. One of his earliest performances was in South Shields in 1871 at the Alhambra Music Hall. When he first began performing, the show was composed of music, but as the years went by he also showcased some of his other talents such as his ability to shoot the heart from an ace of hearts playing card, which he did at one performance at Thornton's Theatre of Varieties in South Shields in 1888. He continued returning to the North East for twenty years, playing to packed halls in Tyne and Wear and always receiving fantastic reviews.

During his career he toured the world, visiting Cuba, Mexico, South America, and much of Europe. When the First World War broke out he visited amputees in hospital to show them it was still possible to live a full life despite the devastating effects of war. At age 65 he appeared in the Danish silent film *Atlantis*, in which a role was created for him. Carl Herman Unthan died in 1929 in Berlin and his biography, *The Armless Fiddler*, composed by Carl himself on the typewriter using his feet, was published some years later in 1935.

ARCTIC EXPLORER

Captain Joseph Wiggins is a name that is not likely to be familiar to many in Sunderland now, but back in the late 1800s it is doubtful you would not have heard of him. Wiggins was a master mariner from Sunderland who would go on to be an internationally recognised Arctic explorer.

In a now largely forgotten feat of bravery and determination, Captain Wiggins set out to pioneer the first establishment of a commercial route through the Kara Sea to Siberia. As a result of his energy and fearlessness he became very well known on Tyneside and recognised by Russia. The Commander of the Marine, at the request of the Czar, presented him with a silver punchbowl ornately engraved with ladles featuring a Russian proverb in old Slavonic characters. He would return to the North East many times, lecturing in halls and telling tales of exploring the Arctic and Siberia as well as to visit his sister. His astonishing gift from the Czar was also exhibited in the shop window of a local man named R.L. Rennison, in Bridge Street, along with the letter he had received from the Russian authorities. His achievement fostered great diplomacy between Great Britain and Russia and opened up a whole new realm of commerce and trade. Captain Wiggins later left the North East and retired in Harrogate, quite possibly telling stories of his adventures on the sea, and perhaps even of his time in Sunderland.

JÓZEF BORUWŁASKI

Born in Poland in November 1739, Józef was a dwarf who was believed to have come from a family of little wealth. Some years later he was adopted and was inducted into the aristocracy of Poland, spending time among the rich and travelling Europe.

Described as being a charming character, Józef travelled all over from Vienna to Paris, and was introduced to noble people across Europe. When he met the former King of Poland, his introduction aroused the jealousy of the court dwarf, who is said to have attempted to throw Józef into a fire on one occasion. When the next King, Stanislaw II, acceded to the throne he took Józef under his protection. However, the King's new bride did not take kindly to him and he was thrown out, with the King continuing to provide a small allowance.

After leaving, Józef got married and began a new tour with his family. This time he made notable appearances in the United Kingdom, even meeting the future King George IV and the rest of the royal family. His allowance eventually stopped and the expenses for his tours tallied up, leaving him with money problems. Unable to make much money from his music, he was forced to display himself for money, something he described as deeply humiliating.

Józef was eventually offered a place to live in Durham with the cathedral organist Thomas Ebdon. Living on the banks of the River Wear, he spent time with his friend, Stephen Kemble, of the famous acting Kemble family and updated his autobiography. Here in the North East he lived out the rest of his life, dying peacefully at the old age of 97, and is buried alongside his friend Kemble. In Durham Town Hall there is a life-size statue of him in remembrance as well as a collection of his clothes and possessions available to view.

ABEL CHAPMAN

Abel Chapman was born in Sunderland in 1851 and came from a long line of sportsmen, hunters and naturalists. His grandfather, Joseph

Crawhall, founded the National History Society of Northumbria and was known for being a crack shot while hunting grouse in Northumberland. As a young boy, Abel would also come to Northumberland to hunt and sketch the birds he saw.

During his youth he travelled the world hunting game and wild birds. Trophies from his hunting trips are on display at the National History Museum in London, Sunderland Museum and Winter Gardens and also across museums in Newcastle. He went on to join his father's firm before leaving to travel as part of his work in the wine trade, seeing Spain, Portugal and Morocco. His conservation attempts saw him recognised as responsible for saving the Spanish ibex, a species of wild goat, from extinction.

After his retirement he visited South Africa in 1899 to hunt big game but was disappointed to find certain areas over-hunted. The Boer War cut his trip short and upon his return to England he drew up plans to protect the Kruger area from further harm by creating a nature reserve. In 1900 his proposals were sent to the International Convention for the Preservation of Wild Animals in London, and shortly after the Sabi Game Reserve was created. By 1903 the park was such a success it was extended and a second reserve opened nearby. Today the reserve is now a core part of Kruger National Park and is considered a tourist hotspot.

Back in England, Chapman had moved to Houxty in Northumberland, where he created his own little nature reserve. His country home and surrounding grounds were designed to attract wildlife, which Abel would sketch. While the idea of a game-hunting naturalist might seem like a contradiction, I am sure people are grateful for his efforts today. Chapman died in Houxty in January 1929.

CATHERINE COOKSON

One of the more well-known characters to come from the North East, Dame Catherine Cookson was born in 1906 in Tyne Dock, South Shields. Known as Katie in her youth, she would eventually move to Jarrow, leaving school at the age of 14 and working in domestic service and in a Harton workhouse.

Growing up, she was the illegitimate child of an alcoholic named Kate Fawcett and was led to believe her mother was her sister. She was raised by her grandparents, something not all that uncommon at the time. Taking up writing as therapy to help her deal with depression, she would go on to write almost 100 books. These eventually sold over 123 million copies, which made her the UK's most widely read novelist at the time.

Many of her novels were adapted for television and her success would see her donate large sums of money to the University of Newcastle, Hatton Gallery and a foundation in her name that continues to make donations to worthy causes to this day.

WHEN ANIMALS ATTACK

You may have to allow a little bit of leeway for this tale as perhaps the local connection is not all that strong, but the story is a strange and weird enough one that I couldn't resist. What animal would you least like to be faced with in their natural habitat with no escape?

For the Japanese on Ramree Island, in present-day Myanmar, which at that time was named Burma, it was the crocodiles that infested the swamps of this island. In the closing days of the Second World War, British and Allied forces mounted an assault on the island from the sea and eventually on land, driving the Japanese inland into the mangrove swamps.

One of those ships that bombarded the Japanese with shells was HMS *Eskimo*, originally launched from Vickers-Armstrongs, at High Walker in Newcastle.

Recognising defeat, the Japanese staged a retreat and fell back into the swamps that were infested with saltwater crocodiles. While this tale has sometimes been regarded as an urban myth, it is recognised by many as the largest animal attack ever on humans, with some counting the death toll of the Japanese killed by crocodiles in the hundreds.

Naturalist Bruce Wright, a British soldier who participated in the battle, gave a description of this event in *Wildlife Sketches Near and Far* (1962), quoted by Frank McLynn:

That night [of the 19 February 1945] was the most horrible that any member of the M. L. [motor launch] crews ever experienced. The scattered rifle shots in the pitch black swamp punctured by the screams of wounded men crushed in the jaws of huge reptiles, and the blurred worrying sound of spinning crocodiles made a cacophony of hell that has rarely been duplicated on earth. At dawn the vultures arrived to clean up what the crocodiles had left … Of about one thousand Japanese soldiers that entered the swamps of Ramree, only about twenty were found alive.

There you have it; urban myth or grim tale of the largest animal attack in history? I will leave this one for you to decide.

CIVIL UNREST

Shortly after the birth of the Church of Jesus Christ of Latter-Day Saints in the 1820s, the Mormon religion began spreading out across the world, sending missionaries to Europe. In the early nineteenth century, a small population of Mormons began growing in Sunderland, and as resentment towards their communities spread elsewhere in the world over the years, Sunderland was no exception. Many of the local people disagreed with their different values, leading to a campaign to drive the Mormon population out of the city.

The reactions to the Mormon Church slowly escalated over time. One report tells how the son of Brigham Young, successor to Joseph Smith, was lecturing in defence of polygamy in Sunderland. The audience are said to have laughed at many of his statements outright and when a member of the public asked a question, which was backed by the other spectators in the room, the service was immediately ended.

A similar instance had taken place earlier at the Victoria Hall in Newcastle when a man named as Elder Bond came to speak before an audience in 1857. This time the audience is stated as being mainly working-class men, one of whom again turned the conversation to polygamy and informed the man it was immoral, much to the amusement of the others there. Bond then sought help from the doormen, declaring that those who came to watch him were 'worse than wild indians'.

The Mormon population continued to grow, however, and baptisms regularly took place at local beaches such as Roker and Hendon.

While there had been instances of confrontation with the Mormon population in the North East leading up to 1912, this was the year everything seemed to reach a boiling point. In March a newspaper article stated that members of the Mormon population had been found guilty of trying to recruit schoolgirls to send to North America, fanning the flames of resentment. In this year demonstrations began taking place, and in April a large number of people gathered outside the meeting house on Tunstall Road, with one or two of the opposition sneaking inside. As the service was closing, one young man made it up to the pulpit and made a vocal protest but was soon escorted outside. Momentum for the movement of ridding the city of Mormons began increasing and there were riotous scenes.

At the start of June, another large group gathered armed with pots and pans and began putting placards on the building next door to a church, with the owner's permission, stating their demands. When no Mormons appeared it was rumoured another service was being held elsewhere, so the mob moved to that location. The group could not access the building here but one young man hopped over the back fence, only to be chased away by a man with a poker. After it began to rain, the crowd dispersed and some moved near to Sunderland's Victoria Hall, where anti-Mormon speeches were given.

While here the crowd heard a shout that a young man who happened to be passing by was a Mormon and he was chased into a tobacco shop. The tobacconist hid him but the angry group stormed the shop, only to be intercepted by a young Jewish man trying to defend the Mormon, leading to him receiving a black eye. That same day another old man was assaulted, allegedly in connection with being Mormon, as well as windows of buildings belonging to other Mormons in Grangetown being smashed.

Following this the Church brought charges against a number of youths who had been throwing stones in May that year. Almost all pleaded guilty and the public was urged to conduct their protests in a legal and peaceful manner. The harassment seems to have forced a large part of Sunderland's Mormon population to leave the city, although some endured the harassment and are still present today.

HELL'S KITCHEN

Hell's Kitchen was painted by Henry Perlee Parker in 1817. The painting depicts a number of famous Newcastle characters and eccentrics from this period gathered in the Flying Horse Pub, which was located in Groat Market. Many of those featured in the painting were mentioned in popular local folk songs and ballads.

On the far left we see Old Judy Dowlings leaning on her stick. Old Judy was the keeper of the Newcastle Hutch, which was a type of strong box used by the town treasurer. She was known for wielding her stick to defend the hutch from those who got too close and it had seen use on more than one occasion. A newspaper report written in 1863 quoted the *Handbook to Newcastle-on-Tyne* by the local historian Dr John Collingwood Bruce, which states that 'some shoulders still ache at the thought of her'.

The man standing behind the table who looks like he has his hands in his pocket is Cully Billy, also known as Silly Billy but actually named William Scott. William lived in St Johns Poor House and was the subject of a number of folk songs and ballads. He lived with his mother, who was said to be 4ft tall and who made her living hawking goods. Both were cruelly ridiculed but William was said to have a kind nature and a good sense of humour.

The man at the forefront playing the violin is Blind Willie, also known as William Purvis. Possibly the most well-known of the eccentrics, he was either born without sight or lost it at an early age. William was a fiddler, performer and songwriter, often being found in many of the local haunts in Newcastle, where he would entertain the regulars for the drinks they would buy him. Always seen without a hat no matter the weather, it is said he became sick of having it pinched by the local boys. Like his mother, who lived to over a 100 years of age, William too died in the St Johns Poor House, aged 80.

Although the original painting was lost, engravings of it have survived and are housed in the Laing Art Gallery.

THE WALRUS AND THE MACKEMS

It is said Lewis Carroll took inspiration for his writing from many places, and included in this was his time spent in the North East.

Carroll had cousins who lived in Whitburn, whom he visited regularly. During his time there he allegedly met a carpenter while walking down the beach. It is also said that he encountered a walrus while in Sunderland, although it is disputed whether this was before the publication of *Alice in Wonderland*.

However, another local connection is that in April 1869 Carroll's sister Mary married Rev. Charles Collingwood. Their home, the rectory at Southwick, now named the Holy Trinity, on Church Bank, has been recognised with a historic blue plaque and there is some evidence that it too once housed a stuffed walrus.

The poem 'Jabberwocky' is also said to have been completed in Whitburn. This was also the home of Sir Hedworth Williamson, a relation of Alice Liddell. Williamson introduced white rabbits into the grounds of his home in Whitburn Hall where Carroll played croquet.

THE BOLDON BOOK

Often referred to as the Domesday Book of the North, *The Boldon Book* is a collection of surveys compiled in 1183 by the Bishop of Durham, at the time named Hugh de Puiset. The Domesday Book is a record of the great survey of England, which was completed in 1086 by order of King William the Conqueror but does not include lands north of the River Tees.

Possible reasons for the Domesday Book's lack of information on the North is that little more than a century earlier William laid siege to the region in the hope of subjugating its peoples in a campaign known as the Harrying of the North. Contemporary chronicles tell of the brutality of this campaign, with destruction being caused on a massive scale through widespread famine brought on by the looting, burning and slaughtering. Considered by some as an act of genocide, the damage done to the North was so great that numerous manors were abandoned and some people were even said to have resorted to cannibalism in order to survive.

BOLDON BOOK

The Boldon Book covered areas in the North East of England that following the Norman conquest were liable to tax by the Prince Bishop of Durham and not directly to the King. Although the book differs from the Domesday Book in its scope and function, it provides an insight into everyday life in the late twelfth century, recording the labour, money, produce and value of the lands in relation to the Bishop. Dues were evaluated at individual levels as well as communal ones, with the book said to contain several amusing and seemingly mundane observations.

The Boldon Book takes its name from one of the earliest entries on the Bishops Manor, which resided in Boldon, and its reference throughout the book in relation to custumal dues 'as at Boldon'. Although the original manuscript has since been lost, four copies exist with the oldest being from the thirteenth century.

LET ME ENTERTAIN YOU

In recent years the North East has borne many a star who not only shone in the UK but went on to cross the pond, where their talents have also been recognised. Take Charlie Hunnam, for example, who went from humble beginnings in *Byker Grove* to being the lead figure in popular series *Sons of Anarchy*. Our history when it comes to the spotlight goes back many years, though, as you will see in this chapter.

LIGHTS ... CAMERA ... ACTION ...

It is plain to see from anyone who lives or even visits the North East that we are lucky to be blessed with some beautiful and idyllic locations. While we may not always have the best weather, there is a diversity to the land here that has attracted interest from across the globe.

Some prime examples of this can be found in the massive film productions we have attracted to shoot here over recent years.

Indiana Jones 5

At the time of writing, the untitled fifth film in the Indiana Jones series has been filming at Bamburgh Castle in Northumberland in 2021, with

Harrison Ford himself having been spotted pottering around Newcastle in his free time.

Avengers: End Game (2019)

The Galilee Chapel housed in Durham Cathedral, as well as other parts of the main building, were transformed into the Asgardian palace on the superhero Thor's home planet, Asgard.

Downton Abbey (2019)

Did you know Beamish Museum became home to over 100 cast and crew members for the filming of the acclaimed movie *Downton Abbey*?

Transformers: The Last Knight (2017)

The bustling streets of Newcastle city centre would see Michael Bay set scenes from his movie here, filming in 2016.

Harry Potter and the Philosopher's Stone / Harry Potter and the Chamber of Secrets (2001 & 2002)

Durham Cathedral doubled as the exterior of Hogwarts in a number of exterior shots in the first Harry Potter movie, as well as being the location at which Harry releases his pet owl Hedwig in *Chamber of Secrets*. Another location that has also made an appearance is Alnwick Castle, in particular the memorable broomstick training scene.

Alien 3 (1992)

Seaham would see David Fincher film some opening shots of *Alien 3* on Blast Beach along the Durham coastline.

From xenomorphs to superheroes and Indiana Jones himself, we have attracted a number of movie sets to the North East, with likely more on the way. While this brief list doesn't scratch the surface of films we have drawn to locations up here, I encourage you to get yourself in front of a keyboard and do some searching to see for yourself some of the other fabulous flicks we have hosted.

FELLING GOES TO HOLLYWOOD

What do Hollywood and Felling have in common, you might be asking yourself? Well, one well-known Hollywood actor was born in Felling, which was included in County Durham at the time, back in 1888.

FELLING GOES TO HOLLYWOOD

Paul Cavanagh, born as William Grigs Atkinson, is an English actor who attended Newcastle Royal Grammar School, before moving to Cambridge to further his studies. A very intelligent man, he studied law and was known to have received recognition for his talents in the fields of mathematics and history.

It seems Cavanagh fell in love with Canada when he travelled over and joined the Royal North-West Mountain Police before returning to serve his country in the First World War. Once the war was over, he continued his travels and at one point arrived in Monte Carlo, where a series of unfortunate spins of the roulette wheel would see him lose $22,000. As in the movies, when our character seems most down-and-out, their luck changes and someone nearby offered him a letter for theatrical recommendations in London. ````

This would be his turning point and he began appearing in British silent films before taking the leap across the pond to the US, where his career took off. Cavanagh is credited as appearing in over 150 films, although he has now been largely forgotten. It would be interesting to know what his opinions of the North East were after a life well travelled in show business.

TO KEEP A FOOL

An interesting entry into St Johns register dating all the way back to August 1589 describes how the Newcastle Corporation employed a foole who had passed away due to the peste, more commonly known the plague. Furthermore, in *Brands History of Newcastle*, Vol. II, the following paragraph gives more detail:

> I think it appears plainly from entries in the town's book of payments, that the fools have been idiots kept at the expense of the corporation. Edward Errington, and John Watson, are both mentioned at the same time.

The description goes on further to detail expenses such as a petticoat and for healing the wounded leg of a kept foole.

While I can't say exactly what the duties of the Newcastle fooles were, if I had to hazard a guess I'd say they were akin to a jester; someone who would use jokes, folk songs and the like to amuse those by whom they were employed. I think every workplace still has one or two of these in their own way.

FRIEND OF THE DOCTOR

Born in Sunderland in 1924, William Russell is an English actor who first rose to stardom by appearing in *The Adventures of Sir Lancelot* on ITV.

Developing an interest in acting at a young age, Russell would help organise entertainment during his national service in the Royal Air Force before moving on to theatre upon leaving. He would then go on to star in *Doctor Who*, appearing in the television show's first two series as the doctor's first male companion, science teacher Ian Chesterton, and one of the first four original cast members. The doctor to whom he was a companion was William Hartnell, and he would go on to be in the series until the penultimate episode of season two, titled 'The Chase'.

He did, however, continue his relationship with the long-running series, voicing audiobooks and filling in the gaps of the lost episodes to which he was integral. While his accent is not akin to that of a North East native, who would have thought that the doctor's first male companion was a Mackem?

EILEEN BLAIR

Born Eileen O'Shaughnessey in 1905, Eileen Blair was born into a working-class family in South Shields. Studying at Sunderland Church High School, a school that would see many talented women pass through its ranks and which only closed in 2016, she soon took a particular liking to the English language and literature, pursuing this at St Hugh's College in Oxford later in life.

FRIEND OF THE DOCTOR

It would be down south that she would meet her future husband, Eric Blair, in 1935. While the name Eric Blair likely does not ring any bells, you will have heard of the pen name he authored books under, which was George Orwell.

Although the couple would not have any children together – as Eileen would later discover this was due to Eric being sterile – they had a very close relationship. This could be seen when she went to join her husband in Spain during the Spanish Civil War, volunteering in a post office.

As the political situation deteriorated in Spain, the couple would be forced to leave the country, with Eileen later joining the censorship department of the Ministry of Information. The Blairs would frequently stay at a property named Greystone, which was near Carlton in County Durham, up to the end of Eileen's life. Sadly, Eileen died in March 1945 in Newcastle during an operation, due to anaesthetic being incorrectly administered.

While Eileen lived an extraordinary life, one part of her legacy that is not as well known is her influence on the writing of her husband. Some believe that his renowned book *1984* took huge inspiration from her and her literary work. Eileen had written a poem in 1934 titled 'End of the Century. 1984', which celebrated the fiftieth anniversary of the school she attended in Sunderland and looked ahead to the centenary celebration in 1984. While the poem itself was written a year before she met her husband, there are themes throughout the work such as mind control, eradication of personal freedom and a police state that are present in his now famous work.

CHRISTINE NORDEN

Mary Lydia Thornton was born in 1924 in Sunderland. Growing up in her childhood home on Chester Road, Mary was the daughter of a bus driver and was educated at Chester Road Primary School and Havelock School. She made her first entrance into show business by performing for the Entertainment National Service Association, singing and dancing at variety shows. Mary was the first entertainer to land on the beaches of Normandy after D-Day.

One Sunday afternoon, while waiting in the queue at a cinema in London, an agent who worked for film director Sir Alexander Korda took notice of her and she was signed on a seven-year contract. With this exciting change, Mary took the name Christine Norden and invented a biography where she was the daughter of a Norwegian sea captain. Described by many as Britain's first post-war sex symbol, Mary pursued a career on screen, appearing first as a nightclub singer in *Night Beat*. Her talent saw her cast in numerous films, with some of her most memorable appearances being in *An Ideal Husband*, *Mine Own Executioner* and *Saints and Sinners*.

Considered a prime pin-up attraction by the public, it was rumoured she had numerous affairs with men and women over the years. After appearing in ten films in five years, Mary left for America in 1952, where she married her third husband and settled in New York. By the 1960s she was on Broadway and made history by being the first actress to appear topless on Broadway in the show *Scuba Duba*.

Mary Thornton passed away in 1988 following complications from heart bypass surgery. She was survived by her fifth husband, George Heselden, and her son, Michael Cole. Following her death, part of the planet Venus was named after her as a tribute to Britain's first post-war sex symbol, thus securing her place among the stars for eternity.

MITCHELL & KENYON

Formed by James Kenyon and Sagar Mitchell, the Kenyon & Mitchell film company was created in the late 1800s and based in Blackburn. Travelling all over the country, the pair captured British life in the Edwardian era as well as producing early fictional narrative films and Boer War dramatisations.

On one occasion in November 1901, Kenyon caught the train to Sunderland following a tip that a huge storm was raging on the North East coast. As soon as he arrived, he travelled to Roker Pier in the hope of photographing the brutal scenes taking place at sea. From the front of the lighthouse it is reported he took over 800ft of pictures before he decided to step aboard a small jetty branching from the pier.

Capitalising on this opportunity, Kenyon moved to the edge of the jetty to get a better view of the wild scene unfolding before him. This quote from an article in the *Sunderland Echo* describes what happened next:

> He had nearly finished and was intent on upon his work when a tremendous wave came along and swept past the cinematographer, and in the backward rush, hurled the camera out of his grasp and very nearly dragged him along with it.

Although he escaped with his life, the day's work was swallowed by the sea. Knowing the value of the film inside, he offered a big reward to anyone who could recover the camera and its contents, which caught the attention of the old lighthouse caretaker. Some grappling irons and hooks were fetched but all that was rescued was the leather case that held the camera.

The following Saturday morning the camera and the more valuable film were washed ashore, battered and useless. It seems that the event had not been a total loss, however, as several children were seen flying cinematograph ribbons around the streets of Sunderland.

THE WORLD'S FIRST DOG SHOW

What has come to be recognised by many as the world's first dog show took place in Newcastle on 28 and 29 June 1859. Held thirty years before the first Crufts, the two-day competition was held in the long-demolished Town Hall/New Corn Exchange.

One of the founders, J. Shorthouse, was a well-known successful breeder and exhibiter of Setters, and the event seems to have been catered to just Setters and Pointers. The event attracted over sixty participants from across the country with a prize for best of breed for both being awarded.

THE WORLD'S FIRST DOG SHOW

Local gun producer William Rochester Pape supplied two shotguns as prizes. The prize for best Setter was awarded to William Jobling of Morpeth, while that for best Pointer went to J. Brailsford of Knowsley in Lancashire.

While this event did not become an annual tradition, another show was held in Birmingham later in the same year that did become a popular event. The competitive passion for such shows spread and evolved from there into what is still seen on television today.

THE WORLD'S LARGEST DOG WALK

Carrying on with the narrative of canine firsts here in the North East, the Great North Dog Walk is internationally recognised as being the largest in the world. Achieving its world record status in 1995, the annual event has been recognised in the *Guinness Book of World Records* eighteen times as it gets larger each year.

The 2022 event was held on The Leas in South Shields on 3 June. Over 30,000 dogs attended of over 185 breeds, helping raise money for charities.

Did you know that the first time Nirvana played in the UK was in Newcastle? The group visited The Riverside in October 1989.

TRAGEDY AT THE THEATRE ROYAL

The Theatre Royal opened in 1866 in the middle of Market Square in Jarrow. One of the most important buildings in the town at the time, crowds would regularly come from all over the North East to see performances there. As the years went by the theatre underwent a number of refurbishments and began screening films alongside theatrical performances in 1898, which would continue into the First World War.

One story from the theatre recounts the suicide of actor William Carriden. After the closing performance of *The Private Secretary* by Eugene Stafford's company, a number of the troupe heard a gunshot coming from the actor's dressing room. Upon opening his door they found him, with a revolver in his hand, dead from a self-inflicted gunshot wound to the head. Carriden had suffered an accident some weeks before and went to the doctor for pain in his head the previous week, although fellow actors had not noticed any changes in his behaviour. The following is a quote from the note left in his dressing room:

There is something in my head that is wanting to get out. The man in Newcastle said I was going to the asylum, or be put under restraint, or have a long rest. I am going to have it.

Carriden's death cast a shadow over Jarrow and the people mourned him. The theatre continued to be used as a cinema and feature theatrical performances. During its lifetime it was rumoured to have hosted performances from Stan Laurel and Oliver Hardy on separate occasions. The Theatre Royal was demolished in 1962 and what was once considered to be the centre of Jarrow was no more.

AN ANGEL IS BORN

Travers John Heagerty, also known by his stage name Henry Travers, was born in 1874 in Prudhoe, Northumberland (roughly 11 miles from Newcastle). His family lived there briefly before moving to Berwick-upon-Tweed, where he initially wanted to be an architect before taking to the stage.

His acting career would take him overseas to the US, where he made his Broadway debut in 1901. The last play he featured in on Broadway, *You Can't Take Me With You*, was his most famous and would go on to be made into an Oscar-winning movie in which Lionel Barrymore played Travers's character. It was not until the advent of sound in film that Travers began to appear on the big screen, often playing strong supporting roles.

Featuring in *The Invisible Man* and Alfred Hitchcock's *Shadow of a Doubt*, to name but a couple, Travers's charm saw him not want for work. In 1946 he starred in *It's a Wonderful Life* alongside James Stewart, in which he played Clarence Odbody, the befuddled but kind-hearted guardian angel. Although the film performed poorly at the box office, its purchase by television networks saw it become a regular feature on the Christmas TV schedule.

Travers retired in 1958 and died in 1965, aged 91. He is buried at Forest Lawn Memorial Park in Glendale, California.

COUNT DRACULA GETS HIS BREAK IN SUNDERLAND

In my humble opinion, every man and his dog claims to have some kind of connection to Bram Stoker's novel *Dracula*. This usually stems from a decrepit castle with a faint connection to the author or a member of his family, with claims hailing from Scotland, Ireland and England, to touch on but a few. But who was the inspiration behind the blood-sucking count we have all come to know and love?

Sir Henry Irving was an actor from Somerset. Born in 1838, he would become popular during the Victorian era, and as his career and reputation grew he would go on to become the first actor to receive a knighthood.

His first steps on this career trajectory were taken in Sunderland, when he made his stage debut at the New Lyceum Theatre in 1856 in a role that was unpaid. He continued in Sunderland, even doing pantomime at one point, until the following year, when he moved to Edinburgh.

The inspiring actor would cross paths with Bram Stoker some years later once his thespian teeth had been cut. From 1878, Stoker worked with Sir Henry at the Lyceum in Westminster. The two would strike up a friendship and it is thought many of the count's mannerisms and behaviour are taken from their relationship, and helped shape the character of Dracula.

While there is most definitely a case for a large part of the character of Dracula being derived from the Romanian ruler Vlad the Impaler, remembered for impaling the severed heads of his enemies on pikes, as far as the inner workings of the vampire go, Irving is widely recognised to have played a part.

The last visit of Sir Henry to Sunderland was in 1904, by which time he was said to be gravely ill. The mayor received him at a ceremonial dinner at which he was presented a handsome casket to commemorate his links with the town. He died a year later in October 1905, and his links to the city are now largely forgotten.

TROUBLE AT HMV

The year was 1979 and punk was the music of choice for many a person in the North East. When the American band The Dickies announced a meet-and-greet at HMV in Newcastle city centre over 2,000 eager fans showed up. The resultant crush was too much for the shopfront window, resulting in the glass that was separating the band from the masses smashing and causing £600 of damage. Police reinforcements had to be called in to stop fans trying to get inside.

ENTERTAINMENT ON SUNDERLAND TOWN MOOR

Town moors all over the country have always been a location for locals to gather and enjoy some entertainment. The public's idea of what is classed as acceptable fun has gradually changed over time, with some of the more grim pastimes left behind in the history books.

One popular source of entertainment in the seventeenth and eighteenth centuries was bull and bear baiting. For this, animals would be made to fight dogs in front of an audience until one of the contenders could fight no more, usually resulting in the creature's death. The last record of this taking place on Sunderland's Town Moor is reported to have been in May 1822, a good few years before its ban in 1835. Other sports such as horse racing, wrestling and archery also took place there.

While some of those sports might seem like less brutal choices of entertainment, they were not without their fatalities. Football was often played on the Moor, and in 1667 one match cost a man his life. Inside the second volume of registers of Bishopwearmouth Parish is an inscription stating that on 15 January of that year, Richard Watson was killed while playing the game.

It can be said that Sunderland Town Moor is no longer the city's centre of entertainment and while we may look back at some of these gory pastimes as horrific, I often wonder what will future generations come to think of our lives today and what we choose to do for entertainment.

Did you know that the village of Philadelphia in Houghton-le-Spring is named after the city in the US? Unlike many other places in the world that have been named after parts of England, such as Newcastle in Australia or the town of Sunderland in Massachusetts, a local colliery owner is alleged to have named this part of the North East after the American namesake. This happened as a result of the American revolutionary war when Philadelphia was captured by the British.

TREASURE HUNTING

In December 1884 the barque *Aurea*, from Sunderland, left the Tyne with a collection of North East treasure hunters on board. As with many stories of buried treasure, it originated with a dying sailor's confession and a tattered map. A ship captain, who was described as being well known to the quayside having traded on the Tyne for many years, was given the information from a member of his loyal crew as he was about to die. The man stated that in his youth he was a pirate and was the last surviving man with knowledge of the location of the now buried stolen loot.

Although the expedition that departed in 1884 was not the first attempt to search for the treasure, it caught the attention of everyone in the county. The names of those involved appear to have been kept out of the public record prior to their departure; however, upon their return some of those involved in the trip were named. Among the crew were a Mr Slater, who was a carpenter from South Shields; Alexander Tate from South Shields; John Atkinson, also from South Shields; and Benjamin Russell from North Shields. Setting sail to an uninhabited island in South America, the men no doubt had high hopes of finding enough riches to make them set for life.

The journey was a long one and when the men arrived problems soon began to arise. Unable to get close to the shore, one member of the crew dived into the sea, risking his life to swim to the shore and allow the men a safer passage. Pleased to see everything as described,

TREASURE HUNTING

the men unloaded what equipment they could and began digging in the supposed location. After tearing away at the ground for a number of days, the men were eventually forced to give up and return empty handed. All the crew returned without fatality, although one letter from Russell falsely described two of the crew dying.

This was not the last expedition to look for this specific buried treasure, however, as British journalist Edward Knight took a crew in search some years later. He also returned empty handed but published a book on the expedition called *The Cruise of the Alerte*, which provides some details on the Tynesiders' journey.

Although fruitless, the story of the *Aurea* expedition captured the attention and imagination of people across the North East, all hoping to be a part of the adventure. The treasure itself may have been claimed by a rogue pirate years before they arrived or even never existed at all, but maybe on an island far away lies gold buried beneath a few feet of dirt.

AN UNFORTUNATE MISTAKE

While we can call the North East home to many unusual blunders over the years, there is one particular one in recent memory that might make you smile.

In October 1971 a South Shields museum was exhibiting a Roman Sesterius coin thought to have been minted between AD 135 and 138. That was until Fiona Gordon, aged 9, happened upon it and pointed out that the coin in question was in fact a plastic token given away by a soft drinks firm in return for bottle labels. This would make the museum's dating almost 2,000 years out.

When questioned on her discovery she said, 'I knew because the firm's trademark was printed on the back.'

A spokesperson for the museum reportedly said, 'The token was designed as a Roman replica. The trouble was that we construed the letter "R" on the coin to mean "Roma". When in fact it stood for "Robinsons", the soft drink manufacturers.'

LION TAMERS

During the 1800s, lion taming was a popular act at many travelling menageries and circuses that chose to pitch their tents in the North East. While some may be familiar with the infamous Martini Maccomo, who performed in Sunderland many times and is buried in Bishopwearmouth Cemetery, there were a number of other famous lion tamers who visited the area.

In February 1888 at Mr Thornton's Theatre of Varieties in South Shields, a young female lion tamer performed under the name Miss Senide. Henriette Willard was born in Vienna in 1866 to a fairly wealthy family and began training animals at a young age. One newspaper report states that while staying with a family friend who kept exotic animals, Henriette climbed into one of the cages and refused to get out until her parents promised to buy her numerous animals. Shortly before her arrival in South Shields, during a performance in Dublin, Henriette put her head inside the mouth of a lioness, which became spooked and ended up attacking her.

One local journalist visited her hotel while she was staying in the area and interviewed her about her experiences. This quote is a response to her being asked about what the lions were fed: 'I feed them on flesh certain days in the week. On other days they have pigeons. They have about a gallon of milk each a day. That is the lioness and panther. The bear will not eat flesh. He has bread, and will drink beer like a man. I mean, he will take the pot in his paws and hold it to this mouth. He is also very fond of sugar.'

Accidents in this occupation were a common occurrence, with frequent reports in the paper relating to acts gone wrong. In Blyth in 1898 a lion tamer named Montano had part of his ear ripped off and his neck severely lacerated, almost killing him. Another report from 1894 tells how lion tamer Martina Bartlett sustained a mauling in West Hartlepool, resulting in his hand and arm being mangled.

African lion tamer Sargano Alicamousa visited Sunderland with Bostock's Menagerie in 1890. Brought to the UK by a Navy officer whom he befriended on St Vincent, Sargano had travelled to Africa and caught cubs to raise and train. As with all of the reviews of lion tamers' performances at the time, Sargano was well received.

At a time when opportunities to travel the world were scarce, travelling shows like these would have provided an invaluable opportunity to see exotic animals. Although the treatment of the animals would not have been up to today's standards, the atmosphere inside one of the smoke-filled tents watching a performer stick their head inside a lion's mouth would have been an experience.

PLAYING THE PIPES

Jamie Allan, also known as James, Jemmy and Jimmy, was a famous piper born in Swindon, near Rothbury in Northumberland, in around 1734. Son to another skilled pipe player, Will Allan, Jamie's skills saw him recognised as very talented from a young age. His mother, Betty, was believed to be connected to a gypsy group, which led many to refer to him as the gypsy piper.

Allan's talents saw him attract attention from people up and down the country until he succeeded in becoming the official piper to the Duchess of Northumberland. Rumoured to have played for royalty, he seemed set to cement his place in history as a famous musician – however, his vices began to get the better of him. His employment with the Duchess ended after two years and he turned to a life of petty crime.

While there are many stories relating to the infamous piper out there, it is hard to pin down what is fact. It is known that Allan deserted the army on more than one occasion having claimed his bounty, making him a wanted man. He is also said to have enjoyed romancing women, gambling and heavy drinking. In 1803 he was arrested for stealing a horse in Gateshead and sentenced to death. However, someone intervened and his sentence was reduced to deportation.

Due to Allan's failing health, he was instead locked up in Durham's House of Correction, beneath Elvet Bridge, and kept there for seven years until his death. Sadly a pardon was actually issued by the Prince Regent but arrived shortly after his death. According to legend, if you are near the cells on Elvet Bridge when it is a dark misty night you can hear the ghostly piper play his tune.

KAP DWA THE TWO-HEADED GIANT

The legend of Kap Dwa is said to have begun in the sixteenth century when Spanish sailors arrived on the beaches of Patagonia in South America. There they found a two-headed 12ft-tall giant that would come to be known as Kap Dwa, and while some versions of the story tell how he was already found dead on the beach with a spear through his chest, the most popular tale tells how he was captured alive and brought on board the ship. Kap Dwa is reported to have been strapped to the mast until he broke free, killing four of the sailors. However, his freedom did not last long as a pike was driven through his chest, killing him.

How exactly his mummified remains arrived in England is unclear, but by the nineteenth century he became part of the Edwardian horror circuit, touring the country as a curiosity. He was passed from one showman to another over the years and was recorded as being at Weston's Birnbeck Pier in 1914, where people were charged tuppence to see him. Kap Dwa was spotted at numerous locations, with some remembering seeing him in person and testifying to his credibility as the body was exposed and no joins or seams were visible. One report even states that in 1930 he was examined by two doctors and a radiologist, all of whom claimed he was real.

In June 1971, Kap Dwa made an appearance in Newcastle on the Town Moor, possibly as part of the Hoppings fair. At this time having your palm read cost roughly 50p, although the cost of viewing Kap Dwa is unknown. Another interesting exhibition from this year was a giant whale, which was showcased on the Town Moor in September. Kap Dwa is also reported to have been spotted in Newcastle in 1999, although it is possible he may have been overseas.

Kap Dwa continued to change hands until he was eventually bought by Robert Gerber and his wife. He is believed to currently reside in Baltimore in the US, where he is housed in Bob's Side Show at The Antique Man Ltd among other curiosities. Whether a successful hoax or a true oddity, the story of Kap Dwa is one that continues to live on.

BOWIE MESSES UP

As part of his Glass Spider tour, David Bowie performed at Roker Park Stadium in Sunderland in June 1987. His support was Big Country and The Screaming Blue Messiahs. A crowd of over 36,000 people turned up to watch, paying £15 each.

Bowie arrived late to the stadium due to his plane being grounded in London. When he finally arrived on stage it is reported he then said, 'Thank you, good evening Newcastle.'

THE CLASH HIT HENDON

In 1985, The Clash set out on a busking tour of Britain, beginning in Nottingham and making their way up north. The Clash were one of the biggest punk bands in the world at the time, although frontman Joe Strummer disliked celebrity and they never played on *Top of the Pops*.

On Saturday, 11 May, The Clash played a gig in Gollums Bar in the Mowbray Park Hotel and the Drum Club in Genevieve's night club. The group also played at The Bunker on Stockton Road, but once it became known they were playing it had to be closed as too many people showed up and The Bunker did not hold a licence for live concerts.

During that same tour they also visited Hendon and made some local friends. Here is the story as told by those who were there:

It was around 2pm, Sunday, May 12th 1985. The Salem Hotel was approaching last orders at the bar and a group of Labour Party activists were thinking about getting a final beer before going home.

We were members of Hendon Ward Labour Party and we had been leafleting that morning to thank local residents for voting Labour in the recent local elections, electing a Labour Councillor and removing the Tory incumbent.

Leafleting usually ended up in the Salem Hotel, where we put the world to rights and discussed what we needed to do to remove Thatcher, the wicked witch of the south.

Last orders were called and then a group of young men entered the bar. I turned to my great friend, Bryn Sidaway, and said, 'My God, it's Joe Strummer and the Clash.' The Clash was my band then and still is – couldn't believe it. We found out that they had a relation in Hendon and they had stayed with him overnight. Bryn (a local councillor), not shy of stepping forward, went over to them, introduced himself, told them they had one of their biggest fans in the corner and would they like to join us – and they did. We were regulars at the Salem and were good friends with the landlady. She agreed to open the bar again and we had a great afternoon swigging ale, discussing politics, the need for change, political activism and music.

Joe Strummer had bright red hair and throughout the afternoon another great friend, Geoff Dodds, referred to him as carrot top. He didn't seem to take offence, particularly as the beer flowed.

At about 3.30 The Salem was keen to close and for us to move on. It was a Sunday afternoon tradition that some of us took turns to cook Sunday dinner for part of the group. That Sunday afternoon it was Geoff Dodd's turn and it was lucky he lived in Upper Flat, 13 Salem Street, which was across the road from the Salem. The roast beef and roast potatoes were already cooking. They were invited and they agreed to join us. The afternoon increasingly took on a party atmosphere and the merrier we got. We shared Sunday Roast beef and roast potato sandwiches and, in return, they offered to play us some of their songs with the basic musical instruments they had. These were supplemented by Geoff's bongo drum and guitar with only 5 strings. They tuned it and used it. I made a particular request for them to play 'Armageddon Time'. They kicked off their set with 'Trailers for Sale or Rent'.

Fortunately, Geoff's son, Steven, had the sense to press the record button on his cassette player, so we have a recording. This is Steven's recollection of the event:

For me that afternoon changed everything about my music and has probably influenced everything I've ever liked since. It started my love of live music – the only thing I've missed during lockdown. I have a vague memory of my dad offering Carrot Top a bottle of whiskey if he could get a tune out of the guitar and I'm sure his Bongo drums were out, too. I can't really remember much else except how buzzing everyone was and singing along encouraged by Carrot Top. Probably the only time I heard my dad singing (apart from at football) and he used to be a decent folk singer from what Linda tells me. The bar I've built is a tribute to the Clash and I called it Rock the Clashbar.

This was the day before my dad's 40th and a week or two before the planned visit of Prince Charles and Lady Diana to a local Housing Co-op. I remember my dad telling Joe about his Republican protest plans and Joe Strummer offering to get hundreds of punks to come and join us.

Word had got around the local neighbourhood that the Clash had been in the Salem and then moved to Geoff's, and a number of children gathered outside and danced throughout their performance.

At 6ish they said they had to move on – they were going to Edinburgh that evening. You can hear on the CD how we tried to persuade them to stay but to no avail. They were gone.

As written by Kevin Marquis, who was there and made a recording, which he has preserved for all these years. A special thank you also to Clive Davis, Geoff and Steve Dodds, Bryn and Kath Sidaway, Susan Stanton, Paul Whiston, alias the Hendon kids.

Armed only with acoustic guitars, The Clash successfully stormed Sunderland, leaving many with fond memories of their interactions with the group.

THE DEATH OF SID JAMES

While performing on stage in a show called *The Mating Season* at the Empire Theatre in Sunderland on 26 April 1976, well-known *Carry On* actor Sid James suffered a fatal heart attack. At first no one could tell if this was a gag, and even when a doctor was requested from the audience he himself believed it to be an act. The doctor called an ambulance and Sid died on his way to the hospital.

When Empire manager Roy Todds phoned the show's producer, Bill Roberton, to tell him the news, Roberton thought it was a joke. 'Sid James has just died in Sunderland,' said Todds. 'Don't worry, everybody dies in Sunderland,' replied the producer.

STOWAWAY

What are you a fan of? Everyone loves something, whether it is a musician, artist, film or actor. Well, I ask you, how far would you go to have contact with that beloved thing in person? The following story is of someone who was willing to go that extra measure.

Let me transport you back to 1966, when there was no internet or mobile phones. Arguably the biggest band in the world, The Beatles, is playing on the radio. If, like myself, you were born well past this era, then it is a hard thing to imagine. Being passionate about something you love, however, is not.

While most of us might be content to simply see our favourite band in person, 12-year-old Carol Dryden, of Springwell, was not. Carol hatched a plan three months in advance to get herself to The Beatles, which involved a 280-mile journey on the railway. How was this guaranteed to get her into The Beatles' HQ, you might ask? Well, Carol had a clever ploy in mind.

Carol and her school friend managed to get a lift in a van driven by her father down to Monkwearmouth train station with a big travelling chest. The two determined girls departed from their chauffeur, taking the case with them down to the platform, at which point Carol was helped inside by her friend.

The 3ft-square box was no doubt cramped even for a 12-year-old girl but this didn't stop her and she climbed into the crate addressed to The Beatles fan club. While tying the crate, the strange sight of a girl trying to load the crate caught the eye of a porter. He placed the crate onto a weighing machine, while her partner in crime paid the correct postage to send the living package down south.

All was going swimmingly until, while waiting on the platform, the porter noticed the crate moving. Carol later said:

> When I got into the box it was turned on its side. I didn't think about food, air or water – only about seeing The Beatles.

Therein was the problem. Trapped in a small box with the air stifling, Carol's wiggling gave her away and the pair's plan was foiled before they had managed to get the box on the train. Luckily so as well, as who knows what state Carol would have been in by the time it reached the fan club.

Now, you might be asking yourself how did Carol's parents not know of this ingenious plan beforehand? Well, that had been thought of as well, with her mother Elizabeth commenting:

> Carol had asked if she could stay with her friend and I agreed. She went out in school uniform and took a haversack containing her jeans and blouse. If I had seen the tea chest going I would have been doubtful.

Our little stowaway had even thought to weigh herself beforehand so she knew how much money to bring to be posted down south on the train!

Later a British Railways Police spokesperson said:

> The girl was very lucky she was discovered on the platform. If she had been put aboard a train it is very likely she would never have been able to meet The Beatles at the end of the journey.

The tall tale of someone posting themselves to a distant part of the world is one that appears to be echoed across time. From the Welshman Brian Robson, who posted himself home from Australia in a box, to the parodies we see in movies, the notion of a person packaged up continues to be entertaining. In this local case, however, the consequences could have been dire.

TONY HAWK & THE TOY DOLLS

If you grew up in the 1990s or early 2000s, Tony Hawk is a name you will be familiar with. From his smash hit video games such as *Tony Hawk's Pro Skater* and *Tony Hawk's Underground*, to the legions of skateboarding youths that praised him on the concrete streets where they would ollie about. For those who are not familiar, Hawk is arguably the most famous professional skateboarder in the world!

How is Tony Hawk connected to us in the North East, you cry? Well pipe down and let me tell you. Talented from a young age, Hawk became a member of the Bones Brigade, a professional skateboarding team founded by Stacy Peralta. He was having a tough time, having struggled through the challenges of being recognised at a young age for his talent and the involvement his father had in the bureaucratic side of trying to get the sport recognised.

In one fateful competition in the 1980s, after criticism that he was only able to perform at Del Mar skate park in California, Hawk entered himself into a competition at Upland skate park, also in California. Starting his run amidst fierce talent, he wasn't on his home turf anymore, and he knew he wasn't guaranteed an easy win. It all came down to the fourth skating run. The Toy Dolls's song 'She Goes to Finos' began playing on the speakers and Tony relaxed, getting into his element, even admitting he was singing along at one point.

Formed in Sunderland in 1979, The Toy Dolls are a punk band who are still together today. Breaking the mould on punk and not taking themselves too seriously with tracks such as 'Nellie the Elephant', the band gradually rose to stardom. With humble beginnings playing in local pubs like The Old 29, they now tour Europe and have an army of fans around the globe, seemingly including Tony Hawk.

Now, now storyteller, you say, surely this is a fabrication? A fib? An outright lie? There is no way a punk band from Sunderland was crossing paths with legendary skater Tony Hawk and helping him win a competition with their jaunty song about Finos, a former Sunderland nightclub, in his youth. Well, I retort, you would be wrong! You can hear it from Tony Hawk, the man himself, in the documentary *Tony Hawk: Till the Wheels Fall Off* (2022).

STUDIO GHIBLI – A TRIP TO TYNEMOUTH

In today's increasingly connected world the enchanting works of Studio Ghibli have become increasingly popular in the West. With movies such as *Spirited Away*, *My Neighbour Totoro* and *Howl's Moving Castle*, audiences from all walks of life have been drawn to the magical worlds these tales inhabit.

Founded in 1985, the name most associated with Studio Ghibli is arguably that of Hayao Miyazaki. While their first film release was *Laputa: Castle in the Sky*, in 1987 the group would also release a number of Manga comics as well, and it is under this umbrella that our two worlds will collide.

Born in 1929 in North Shields, Robert Westall was a talented author who published his first novel, *The Machine Gunners*, in 1975, which would go on to be adapted for television by the BBC. Westall would set many of his books in the local areas in Tyneside, such as Tynemouth and Cullercoats, and his story 'Blackham's Wimpy', which made up part of a spooky anthology titled *Break of Dark*, was no exception.

While exactly how Miyazaki stumbled across the North East writer's works is unknown, but he would go on to adapt 'Blackham's Wimpy' in his own unique way. The resulting Manga comic, *A Trip to Tynemouth*, was released in 2006, the cover of which would feature a depiction of Tynemouth beach.

In one section of the story a young Miyazaki visits Tynemouth in search of Westall's ghost and shares a number of details on British bombers in the Second World War, as well as touching on details from 'Blackham's Wimpy'.

While it is unlikely that we will ever see an on-screen adaptation of this comic book by Studio Ghibli, the impact a North East writer has had on Miyazaki and Studio Ghibli is undeniable.